How to be a Summer Dad

Liam Black

Illustrated by Caroline

*I would like to express my sincerest thanks to the staff of
Guildhall Press for their assistance in producing this book.*
Liam Black

Published in June 2003 by
GUILDHALL PRESS
Ráth Mór Centre, Creggan,
Derry BT48 0RP
T: (028) 7136 4413 F: (028) 7137 2949
www.ghpress.com info@ghpress.com

© Liam Black / Guildhall Press

ISBN 0 946451 73 7

Supported by the Arts Council of Northern Ireland.

This project is supported by the European Union, administered by the
Local Strategy Partnership for the Derry City Council Area.

All rights reserved. No part of this publication may be reproduced or transmitted in any form or by any means, electronic or mechanical, including photocopy, recording, or any information storage or retrieval system, without permission in writing from the publisher. The book is sold subject to the condition that it shall not, by way of trade or otherwise, be lent, re-sold or otherwise circulated without the publisher's prior consent in any form of binding or cover other than that in which it is published and without a similar condition including this condition being imposed on the subsequent purchaser.

To the six:

Rebecca, 15
Thomas, 13
Peter, 12
Stephen, 9
Sarah, 6
Emma, 6

That you might enjoy.

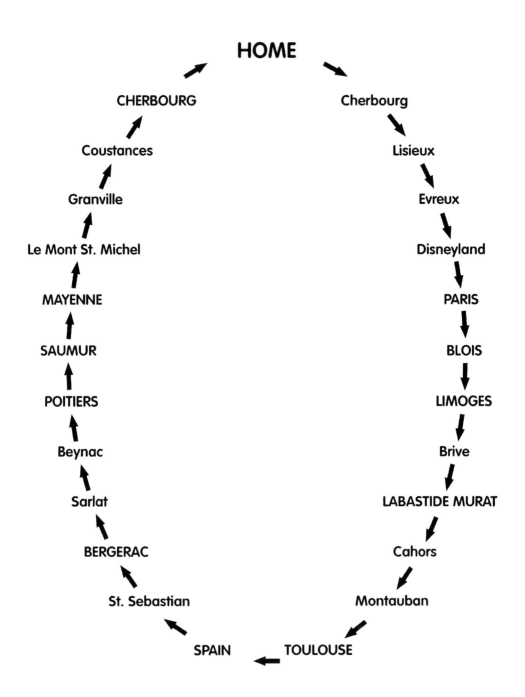

Contents

Chapter	Page
1 Going There	7
2 Getting There	15
3 Being There	20
4 French Heaven	28
5 Hills and Valleys	37
6 Getting Hot	42
7 Spain in a Day	46
8 Settling In	51
9 Getting to Know	60
10 Mixing	70
11 Last Orders	88
12 The Way Back	106
13 Return	125

Chapter One

Going There

The first thing you need is children, the next is summer; that said, go to it.

I am told it has been along time coming. Then again I am told a lot of things by a lot of different people. It is seventeen years since I last had a holiday and to some people this act of inaction borders on the insane. They could be right. I have viewed a lot of holidays as bordering on the insane. We could both be right. July was the month, south of France was the destination and whatever the year Caroline and I were off on honeymoon.

Honeymoon is when two newlyweds are packed off on their lonely twosome to somewhere they've probably never seen before with the remit they get to know each other better than they've already got to know each other. It is a nice idea but in reality it is a hangover from an age when there was meaning in what people did not to mention what they said. Nowadays the act of sex is the only form or expression of religion that a lot of people have, it is their way of keeping in touch with God. Because of this then I am back from honeymoon and before I know it there are six interesting looking faces sitting around the dinner table and they're all calling me, dad. Somehow seventeen years have passed and, like the hair on top of my head, there's no accounting for where it has gone. Sure, there are tangible proofs that we have wandered through them, the children for instance and a few lumps of bricks and mortar. What I have to look back on is a simple sentence 'I worked hard'. That's it. I haven't highlighted my children's memories with 'the year we went to' or 'the time we saw and did.' My children couldn't start school again in September and say: "My dad's a real hard worker and we didn't go anywhere."

I wonder what they did say.

Holidays are something to look back on as proof of having lived.

Holidays are something to look forward to, to talk about, to enjoy at least once a year for the majority and as the need arises for a growing minority. Expectation is obviously a large part of the holiday game, expectation backed up by hard earned cash will certainly give you something to look forward to and which you will have convinced yourself is going to be absolutely wonderful, the time of your life for now anyway. You have weeks, maybe even months, to convince yourself through the reactions of others that what you are doing is wise, desired, perhaps even an enlightened thing to do; but this of course is not the case for me.

What's ahead of me is a six-week trek away to foreign parts in an air-conditioned Volkswagen Caravelle with wife and six. We'll come back to numbers later. In my head the holiday is a big adventure for the eight of us. It marks a kind of denouement where I leave my old worked out self behind and return from foreign travels a better, wiser, relaxed, smiling, loving, understanding, happy husband, father, son, brother and friend to my relative mix. I should have left out smiling here as it's the one thing I've always retained despite the many years of hard business life topped off with high active home life. I think it must have been a nasal impediment kept me smiling.

What will it do to me? Who will I be when we come home?

Knowing the little I know of myself I reckon nothing much will have changed except perhaps developing the ability to spent money instead of going out every day to try and earn some. Judging by the way many others appear to live their lives these days perhaps it would be more cost effective to spend money rather than save it; not that saving money was an option with the demands of six young mouths and a big house. I don't smoke these number of years, have never drank, don't bother with the social scene. I enjoy the company of the few be it in their home or ours or out somewhere decent for a bite to eat, just so long as it's good people in good surrounds, eating and chatting the hours away and the rest of the happy gathering can drink to their merry contentment as I'll always drive the gathering home.

Which leads me to thinking of food and the wonderful necessity of eating abroad. I'm looking forward to lots of fresh breads, fruit and glorious meals eaten in and eaten out; to a more relaxed attitude to eating every meal of every day; to enjoying the company of my children as we take time out from our home selves; to having the chance to breathe different air with the hope of a less frenetic heartbeat. The driving I don't mind at all, it should be straight forward enough although I know I'm saying this from a blind perspective since I've never driven on the continent before. Hey, it can't be that bad. I've heard all the stories of mad drivers on the continent and how they have no thought for anyone else on the road, that the drivers in Paris are the worst and whatever you do don't go near the Arc de Triomphe because no insurance company in the world will cover you for driving in any of its meandering lanes. I'm up for it all, and if anything should go wrong I've got a good co-driver to point the finger at.

With regards work, and this always spills over into family life, I have felt for the past couple of years that I have been running on empty. I worked very hard at business and then because of changes in government duties I had to work even harder at the business for a lot less money. Business people are the eternal optimists and to this end we understand that there are bad days in business just as there are good, there are bad seasons just as there are good, there are bad years just as there are more bad years was the situation. You keep going and going though thinking that things will change that they cannot remain as bad as they are. After seven years it dawns on you that this is it, this is how it is going to be unless you do something about it. It is not up to anyone else, it is up to you, either you change things for yourself or you don't. Stop crying about it even if this is just to yourself; stop making life miserable for yourself and less than absolutely wonderful for those closest to you and do something about it.

Two years ago I decided to do something about it and it has taken two years of hard work to structure the thoughts into plans onto paper and thence into reality. I have added more units for rent onto the business and decided to rent the whole lot out. At this stage it's well on the way to being sorted. This then is the work end more or less taken care of and now what I have to find out is whether there's a living breathing person still alive within this shell of a worker. In our break with past we're off on our break. A few days time will see us leave the house at around six in the morning, drive three hundred odd miles to catch a ferry at four in the afternoon which is to take us across to Cherbourg and a new life, a new way of being for a short time at least.

We are to arrive in Cherbourg around midday the following day and thence onto Paris for two nights. The one full day in Paris is to be spent in Eurodisney and I can say with a great amount of certainty that I am not looking forward to this.

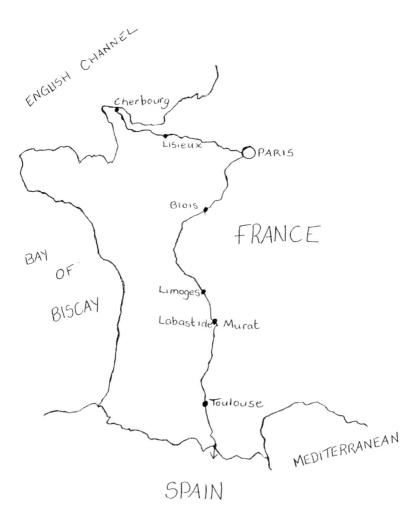

Getting packed looks like a stressful time. Clothes, shoes, passports, money, tablets, creams, not to mention what suitcases to take, bags to bring, even down to what grade of black plastic bag to take. You name it, it's going on holiday with us. What is most amusing or annoying if you are silly enough to let little things get to you, are the fanciful ways and notions that some of the family have. Maybe it's over indulgence on the part of their mother which might sound a bit sore coming from someone who takes a very back seat when it comes to active involvement in the rearing of his children but, I've always believed that life is simple when you keep it simple. Let me explain.

I wear white pants. Not something you might want to know. Certainly not something you need to know. There it is plain and simple. The reality of this is I do not have to go searching through wardrobes and drawers to find colours which match colours, nor do I have to try and find colours which don't make a spectacle of themselves in light summer clothing. Simple.

Then there's deodorant. Whatever's sitting on top of the dressing table is what I put on. It can be pink, it can be blue, it can be rancid green in colour, it can even smell like a perfumery for all I care. My sweet smelling little darlings are so indulged by their mother that I can hear "I only wear...!" I must question them to see if any are being sponsored by a deodorant company, I could be missing out on something big here. Judging by the smell of the boys sometimes I wouldn't be surprised if they were being sponsored by an after shave company even though the older two boys only shave about twice a year; at other times as they pass in their school uniforms instinct tells you to breath in twice to be certain that the dung smell passing you was unfortunately real. Perhaps this is all a necessary call of individuality in a household of many where the six are too often made to function as one homogenous unit. Why should I care? I'm not into indulging myself not to mention indulging any of my children.

Caroline has it all to do and she does it with a smile on her face. It's the morning after tomorrow morning we're off and I made a simple tea of bananas and salad and breads. Caroline, after quickly scoffing hers, jumped up and chirped:

"Must get back to it."

In fact, just to let you know what a really wonderful fella I am, I made dinner as well. Yes, really. That is if you regard heating a bolognese mix, boiling water with spaghetti in it, placing two supermarket bought pizzas in a hot oven and releasing a load of frozen chips onto oven trays as cooking. Yes, I have my doubts too, goodness certainly doesn't come in small or large packets, it is more akin to bulking our stomachs. The deskilled elements of my cooking ability are borne out of necessity and not a wish on my part to wear a white hat and throw tantrums in the kitchen; the reason for cooking any dinner goes back a bit, perhaps nine years.

The past nine years of running a petrol station existence has meant that I have worked every Sunday morning, normally managing to quit my post at between one and two in the afternoon. Caroline has thus long regarded herself as an ecclesiastical widow first with three, then with four and finally with six children she went to church every Sunday "on her own" as she often repeated to me. This then was the long awaited first Sunday in nine years Caroline would have a husband on show with her to prove to the whole world she was not a woman rejected, neglected or on her own. Very happy she was about this. Until the Saturday night before when Sarah, one of the six year old twins, decided she had a toothache and was she ever right; she had a rotten pit in the middle of one of her first tooth molars. The little darling had been to the dentist around a month ago with the beginnings of a problem in this same tooth only for the dentist in his wisdom-toothed head to announce that 'it's best to leave well enough alone'. Well enough was left alone but well enough didn't leave little Sarah alone. Back then to one of the dentist's underlings last week who prescribed an antibiotic and virtually pushed Caroline and Sarah back down the stairs with a plenitude of condolences. The antibiotic was acquired in powdered form to be made up whenever real need arose which, as we all know would most probably be while we were away on holiday. Saturday night then had the poor child up crying with the pain of the rotten tooth a number of times until a cotton bud dipped in clove oil and pushed firmly into the piece of nasty in her tooth did the trick; relief came soon for Sarah and thence to sleep.

As luck would have it, or not, depending on whether you are the dentist, or not, the dentist on call for the area this weekend proved to be none other than our young colleague of the non-event of before. You could see the enthusiasm of his weekend doings drain from his face as immediate memory brought to the forefront of his mind the prospect of what he now had to do. He could see there was no way out of this one, that this Sunday morning brought the joy of extracting himself from his recent non event, ourselves from the threat of a lot of ennui in France and a big double brute of a tooth from my poor little darling's mouth. He gassed her, jagged her, pulled and pulled again, gauzed her, stickered her and then we were back out the front door of the surgery in the street, in the wagen and away. All this while Caroline was unfulfilling her long cherished ambition not to be the merry Mass widow with the rest of the clan.

I'll bet the tooth fairy is generous with this one.

I keep advising the kids that this is high stress time for their mother and so they are to help help help and not answer back. I keep asking Caroline if there is anything I can do but the answer remains firmly the same:

"No, I'm doing brilliantly on my own."

I don't know what made me delude myself into thinking I could be of help. At the moment pink Barbie swimming armbands are being deflated to a size compatible with coming away with us; electric fans, small bendy scissors, tweezers, in fact you name it and I bet we'll have it away with us.

As well as the problem of what to take away with us there is the associated problem of what's left behind. Jewellery and stash are taken out and relocated in a safe house; inlaws are in charge of taking in the post, looking after the goldfish and the other one that used to be gold but has been demoted to a secondary silver, and tending to the needs and requirements of Stephen's tomato plant; brother Tom, who lives a few houses behind, will keep a close eye; nephews are engaged with doing rounds of the garden and making sure that my plums are intact; other friends have dedicated their whole lives to patrolling in and around our garden walls.

In less time than it takes to hard boil an egg, Thomas and my eager self had the wagen packed with cases, bags, black plastic bags, fans (I'm not overly fussed at the prospect of sitting in an air conditioned fridge

for long periods of time) bottles of water, bottles of orange juice, toilet rolls, kitchen rolls, hand wipes, face wipes, cameras, camcorder, binoculars, sandals, shoes – we packed, layered, pushed and squeezed in. In the meantime I think I'll keep out of the way, Caroline's stress level has passed boiling point and is still rising. God knows what the next few days hold because I cannot see Caroline's eyes having anything but a manic stare until after we leave Paris. Spending a full day in Eurodisney, looking after and trying to entertain six youngsters, not to mention the effort to get everyone out there and back in safety, will no doubt do wonders for both our blood pressures.

Chapter Two

Getting There

'Normandy' is the name of our pleasure cruiser so God knows what sort of a landing we'll have. I joke, about the 'pleasure cruiser' bit anyway. It is twenty years old and I reckon sea-faring terms are akin to doggy years so multiply by five or seven or whatever it is and that will give you an idea of the scale of luxury we're steeped in. Add to this the fact that our cabins are in the bowels of the ship and you are a bit nearer the truth of it; we are obviously not too far removed from the ship's engine judging by the associated smells and noise. It's easy to complain though, too easy when you are away out of your normal way of working and are dipping your toes into the ways of the common traveller for the first time, then there is going to be an awful lot to complain about.

There haven't been many old sea dogs in our family background. The only one I can think of is an uncle of my grandfather's on my father's side who supposedly went down with all hands on a merchant ship during world war one. A bit of rowing in my youth I don't think will account for very much. I think therefore I'd better hold my tongue till I see how it all pans out.

The couple of hundred odd mile journey from home to port was relatively uneventful save for the chance sighting of a coupling pair of cows, or a cow and a bullock, or whatever way it works. The rest of the journey was scenery or was it that the rest of the scenery was journey? I think perhaps it depends on how intent you are on your driving. The most noticeable feature of the journey was that we drove through so many towns; real live thriving places of work and living that have managed in good part to ignore most of the consequences of living in the latter part of the twentieth century.

Up around where we live towns don't seem real any more, they retain somewhat of their original shape but that's about the height of it. They function merely as dormer towns where all age travellers commute to and from their places of work. They have not retained the full array of shops and places of workmanship which are necessary to sustain a community. Perhaps 'community' is an old age notion which if it ever really did exist does not show itself much among the urbanites of nowadays. Individuality is all the rage now, everything and everyone is judged in terms of the self, in terms of the 'what's in it for me?' attitude. Forget about a person feeling part of a family which is part of an extended family which is part of a church which is part of a community which is part of a society which elects leaders to promote and protect its collective and thereby everyone's self interest. Individuals being the building blocks whilst the mortar was their collective self-interest and together this made up the communities of the state. Sight of this, need for this, dependence upon this, appears to have been lost to a majority of what were formerly known as citizens, who have been blinded by the glut of goodies of the modern age. The fact that most of these goodies are bad for you as a nation state is something for another page. I have digressed long enough.

This ship of twenty years is slowly heaving its way over calm waters so that by early afternoon tomorrow we'll be disembarking onto French concrete and tar in Cherbourg at the northern tip of the country. There were hundreds of cars, vans, caravans, caravanettes, trailer homes, boats, motorbikes, bicycles, not to mention the thousands of people. They are quite literally crammed in. So much so that a seriously fat person would have no option but to sit in their vehicle in the cargo hold for the entire sea journey. There is no possible way a big fat bouncy person could make it out of the cargo hold so tightly packed are the vehicles. If one did manage to blubber his way out and escape into the sleeping quarters he would have just enough room to collapse on the floor so that others in the cabin would have to jelly up and over him for there is no chance on God's lonely earth that he could fit into one of the bunk beds and breathe at the same time.

Let me now say if ever I need measured for a coffin and I suppose there is a realistic chance of this happening sometime in the far and I hope very distant future, then the undertakers need look no further than one of these bunk beds. It is based on a very original design from around two hundred and fifty years ago when slave ships were all the rage. I suppose nothing much has changed except nowadays we are slaves to our own greed, to others' expectations, to the need to be constantly changing, acquiring, improving, getting, buying, spending, spending, spending whereas heretofore the slaves were simply objects of the greed of others. It must be time to go to sleep. I'm going to try to go to sleep now. I'm going to try to go to sleep now. I'm going to try to....

I tell you, it's amazing what you can do if you are tired enough; I slept all-night and so did the boys. Thomas even had to be wakened at a quarter to eight this morning. Despite plenty of quarter turns on the bed I feel thoroughly rested and ready to hit the road. There was only one interruption during the night when there was a thud followed by some gentle crying emanating from the cabin next door. The cabin next door was occupied by Caroline and the girls and it turns out that Sarah, in her tender wisdom, decided to lie the wrong way round on one of the top bunks; fortunately she landed on her hands and knees and was none the worse for her experience as soon as she calmed down.

Some people seem remarkably well suited to ship life and I'll bet the closest they've come to a sailor being in their background is an old pair of bell bottoms. Whilst myself and family play cuckoo with our cabin doors as we nip out quickly across the couple of feet of corridor to use the toilet and have a quick wash, these high sea pirates stand about, cool as you like, obviously just having come out of the shower. Mind you last night there were mothers and children lying sleeping on the floor of the corridor outside our cabins; I suppose they were safer and warmer lying down here than they would have been on the communal floors above. Perhaps there wasn't enough room for them above for there were a lot taking the cheaper option.

Today, thankfully, Caroline's equilibrium appears to have returned to her after her superb imitation of a drunk woman yesterday as the ship got going, she nearly had the shirt ripped off me while we were performing our comedy walkabout for the benefit of the many smiling seafarers. Apart from the open of the top deck, it was not easy finding an empty seat for Caroline to try and settle herself last night with the boat being so packed and the quick, smart, voyagers having nabbed any chair or seat they could to sit out the journey. The cinema was our only means of hope and here we passed an uncomfortable enough couple of hours watching Big Fat Liar but at least it did the job it was meant to do because it broke the back of the journey before sleep took care of most of the rest.

It's a good thing we were up and about relatively early this morning as there are now excruciating queues along the corridors for the communal toilets.

I am functioning brilliantly without a watch so far, it helped me sleep better last night; my decision to leave my watch behind is based on the fact that my life has been run by time for what now seems like an eternity. Not only do I want to end the rule of the watch but also that fascist little instrument, the alarm clock, which took great delight in cancelling out my dreams at six o'clock in the morning, God knows how many mornings every week. My latest watch, which arrived on my birthday last year from Caroline, looks and acts every bit the part that a watch should. It is automatic, which is my preferred kind and it has luminous hands, which has meant that for the past year now any night I woke up during my sleep I ended up staring deliriously at my left wrist in a great effort of sub-conscious consciousness to try to ascertain exactly what time it was I was not asleep at. It is very confusing. In the great scheme of things it is about as necessary as having a mistress, it may seem like a good idea but when reality bites there are two women holding onto your shirtsleeves to keep their balance instead of one. Anyway, Stephen is never far from me and he has been nominated official timekeeper for the family for the duration of the holiday.

Breakfast is the next duty of confusion we are about to embark upon. Fruit and juice is all that is deemed necessary for breakfast, not I suspect through any life changing attitude toward healthy eating but rather by way of the unhealthy attitude of some of the stomachs. Up on deck we go and soon we have our first sighting of land since leaving our fair shores. Alderney it is and very heart warming too to see this the most northerly of the Channel Islands.

I think it was Victor Hugo called them:

"Little bits of France dropped into the sea and picked up by England."

Little shittings off England which a lot of tax redundant fleas have congregated on is probably more the truth of it nowadays.

Next we sight Cherbourg about which there is nothing remarkable as it is a city which has settled nicely into an ordinary piece of French coastline, except for the ship's captain's final announcement that: "Cherbourg has the largest nuclear reprocessing plant in Europe." Definitely not the place to go to for a swimming holiday.

Chapter Three

Being There

I suppose the French are used to invasions of all sorts, from the friendly to the not so friendly kind, so I doubt whether they'll notice another boat load of sunny hopefuls disembarking onto their hallowed right hand drive roads. The French countryside along the back roads we are driving from Cherbourg to Lisieux to Evereux to Paris is sunny and beautiful. The houses are just as they must have been fifty, one hundred and more years ago. The fields around are probably a lot bigger than a century ago but their crops are wonderful looking, tall and healthy as they sway lightly in the warm summer breeze. Their good health puts our own farmers' feeble efforts to shame but our eating habits would put theirs to shame, there's not a potato field in sight. I cannot imagine what a dinner plate would look like without a spud of some cooked form on it.

These secondary roads or whatever it is we are travelling on are a peculiar expression of French psyche in that most governments we know like to tell us what speed we should be doing when we are driving. The French drivers are not only shown when to overtake but where to overtake and this fine feat of French officialdom rotates who exactly can do what every five miles or so. At the end of each of these five mile rotations there are special little breakdown areas if the exasperation of having been overtaken proves too much for the poor French drivers.

Paris is – immense.

See Paris and drive.

The trick to successful driving in Paris is that you very quickly become one of them. As the saying goes: 'When in Paris, do what the Parisians do – drive like a maniac!'

Rapid acceleration, shooting in in front of traffic going in what appears to be your direction, always remembering to indicate your intentions afterwards. It is absolutely brilliant, so much fun. The French, I suspect, have been practising this for many a long year in anticipation of my arrival. As for finding our destination in the centre of

Paris this was very straightforward; as with almost everything else in life success comes as a matter of course after you have exhausted all the unsuccessful alternatives. One hundred and eighty-degree turns are easily accomplished on Paris' vast boulevards just so long as you remember to ignore the driving aspirations of other motorists.

I cannot help but think how much better at it the French are and when using 'it' I would like it to be considered all embracing. By way of an example is the fact that for the past nine years I have toiled at my filling station cum shop cum car wash to the extent that I, along with so many like-minded morons throughout the country, have closed on just one day each year, Christmas Day. I know this may make us seem like a very selfish, unreasonable and not a very public spirited lot by doing our customers out of their need to go out spending every day but we are learning. Imagine the size of the smile on my face after we passed quite a number of filling stations with a rope or chain across each entrance and a sign up stating: 'Closed 14th July. Re-Open 5th August.'

That's what I call being independent. The oil companies have not yet managed to squeeze the retailers into a corner in France such as the one we must sign up to at home which requires us to be open a minimum of fifteen hours each day but it does allow for our closing one day each year. The retailers for their part still possess enough good sense and margin to go off and enjoy the considerable blessing they are fortunate enough to live in the midst of.

For my own part and for the vast majority of small businesses, I have to say holiday time was always a nightmare. When staff took their well earned two week break in the summer or indeed their winter break it meant your poor hard worked body had to work even harder. Other members of staff could sometimes be enticed into covering some of the day or night shifts with the lure of extra cash but the reality was that their holiday entitlements had to be covered as well. At the end of every holiday period, be it summer or Christmas, physical and mental exhaustion had set in so that what you needed more than anything else was a holiday but this was the last thing on earth you could manage. The knock-on effect of this is that at home you were even less of a help than you normally weren't; you were short-tempered as well because of your over overwork and lack of sleep. Not only did you not have the time to indulge your family in happiness but you now lacked the inclination as well and these, as we learn all too often afterwards, are the most special times for children to get hold of their father and learn from him and teach him as we all enjoy each other's good company.

The really sad thing is that I knew all of this at the time. I also knew it was not important enough to make me flinch from my duty as father provider. My duty first and foremost was to run my business so I could successfully provide for my family, therefore there was absolutely no chance I was going to fail in my duty toward my business and hence toward my family. The fact I worked very hard meant that I expected those close to me to have the same hardened attitude towards leisure time as I had; what a bundle of fun I must have been.

In Paris the underground car park near our hotel is situated between the street and the footpath, the only way to describe it is that it just shoots down from the level of the street and with a sharp right hand turn it disappears. If the overhead sign at its entrance is to be believed it is 1.85metres high, I hope this is correct, in fact I hope this is precision correct because the handbook on our Caravelle states that it stands 1.84metres tall on the level but there is a sharp drop from street level down into the underground parking. This could tip the balance in favour of the grey concrete above the entrance. Both the French and the Germans are precise in their measurements, we had at least a couple of millimetres to spare. Tomorrow morning we are away to Eurodisney but for the moment we are off out to find something delicious to eat as well as trying to find the metroline to see if we are anywhere near route A which will take us to Marne-la-Valtee where we disembark to meet Mickey and his host of friends.

We left our hotel rooms and armed with our map of Paris we headed off in the right direction and we walked and walked and walked, and walked and walked and walked. All I can say is that Paris is not big, it is, well, take a metropolis the size of London and you may as well double it, vast in the extreme; therefore what looks like no great distance on a small map turns out to be an enormous distance in reality. Back home we walk mountains for pleasure but over here you very quickly learn to take the metroline everywhere. We were trying to find Gard du Nord station for the train link along the A4 track to Eurodisney but would need a couple of switches on the metroline from our hotel to get to Gard du Nord in the first place.

I have to keep reminding myself that we are going to Eurodisney because I cannot exactly say I have been looking forward to it. Whilst I do like the effect it appears to have on the young and whilst I love the absorbingly playful effect of most of its cinematic creations, I cannot absorb the concept of it being a living, breathing fantasy creation. I know my children will love it to bits and Caroline as well; I know they know it is not real; I know they will have real and happy memories which will stick with them for the rest of their days; but there's something twisted inside my head that will not or cannot agree with it all. I'll grow up some day and accept the world for the way it is, not for my own mistaken narrow-minded view of things.

Dinner tonight eventually came after our extra long walkabout and it was in a pizzeria just a few doors down from our hotel. The restaurant owner's English was poor which was good because it meant he was not the type to go pandering to the wants and needs of tourists; his French was very good which was good because it meant his product was good enough to maintain his business in its high profile position; his Italian was excellent which was very good because Italy is the home of pizza making and chances are he had brought time honoured skills and recipes with him. As expected then the pizzas were beautiful (I have to admit here that our family has been involved in the pizza making business at home for the past number of years so this was a bit of a fact finding mission) thin based and topped with excellent quality product; the surroundings were wonderfully authentic Parisien/Italian and they had the good sense to serve us our minerals as soon as we ordered so that by the time the pizzas arrived we were all ready for a second drink.

Needless to say we all slept like logs that night; it was a good days work well done and when you are well fed and watered your head very quickly melts into the pillow.

We have started out on our big adventure as I like to consider it or our summer holiday as Caroline and the children prefer to refer to it but I don't know if I'll ever grasp the concept. So far it has been a mixture of high miles, high sea, high drama, high-speed, high tension, high adventure, high expense and sheer determined hard work; I wouldn't want to find out what a bad day was like.

Disneyland Paris, as my mother would say, is a stupid place. It no longer wishes itself to be known as Eurodisney perhaps this is because of too close a word association with the Euro which equates with money and Disneyland is not a place you go to to get money. Whatever it's called it is full of people looking for a smile but someone should tell them they're looking in wrong place, they should try looking inside themselves not outside. Anyway, Disneyland Paris is packed full. Packed so you couldn't walk straight. Packed so full of people you had to queue and queue and this was with us being smart and making sure we had the fast track tickets to pass by the longer queues.

Disneyland Paris is packed full with every breed and species known to man, well, all that is except one. White, yellow, pink and every variety of brown dressed as over politely or impolitely as you like; there were even quite a few woman dressed as black pillar boxes with two big dark eyes staring out of each – maybe there were only a couple of them but they kept moving around a lot – which makes me wonder how they fare with their passport photographs. The one major exception is black people. There was any number of young black males and females working in every tiresome, boring, menial job in Disneyland but, apart from a few mixed marriages or mixed race relationships, there were no black visitors at all. Why is this? How come every mixed blessing from every corner of the globe is happy to place his hard earned where his child's mindset is?

When you think back it doesn't take a genius to work out that Disney's best pictures were made when black people weren't getting a fair

crack of the whip, as many Americans might have seen it or perhaps they were, as many Americans might have seen it. Whatever the answer is, the reality is they weren't there and this is something the big boys in Disneyland will have to get their collective head into. My feeling is they already know all of this and they don't care enough to have to do anything about it; with numbers the way they are they are probably working on their next projects which will be Disneyland North Pole and Disneyland South Pole.

As a big feature attraction for this part of Europe not just for this part of France, especially when you calculate the amount of money it generates, I'd say that if the bosses of Disneyland wanted there would be very little hesitation in making Disneyland a principality, although for marketing and advertising purposes I'd say a princessipality would work a lot better. It's the biggest money spinner I've ever come across; okay, so I haven't been or seen too much in the recent past, but I did follow Michael Palin around on all his exploits.

The highlight of the day for me was the metroline we used to get to and from Disneyland. It is efficient and easy to use once you work out how it functions. Once you learn where you are and where you are going to it is the easiest thing in the world to then determine your switch over points. It is fast, efficient and therefore packed to the gills.

With Disneyland now under my belt and the ease this brings I have to say that although it is an expensive stop there is nothing cheap or shabby about the place and there is an enormous amount to do and see, so much in fact I doubt whether half could be visited with their preferred two day ticket. To be honest it is a masterful creation and it is not a multinational venture which has used its big bucks to despoil the French countryside, oh no, it is much bigger and more subtle than that. What the thousands if not tens of thousands of visitors each day are biting into is an enormous slice of Uncle Sam's American Pie. This pie, it is true, has been laced with something but not with anything bad, that supposedly went out with the Cold War. It is instead laced with something that is good for you but it is only good for you so long as you are smart enough to keep it in proper measure. This American Pie is laced with sugar, American sugar, not the protected European stuff. This, to me, is so sweet it is unpalatable but as with drinking diet Coke and ordinary Coke if there's nothing else around you can put up with it, only so long as it is in the extreme short term.

By now the pictures have developed into memories and these in turn have been transmitted into the brain cells of the children which deal with these matters. I'll try to get these brain cells to move over a bit tomorrow morning when we take the Paris underground the short distance to the Eiffel Tower.

Just as we enjoy spending our life filling it out with frivolities; just as we like to fill our diet with a greater and wider variety of lovelies; so it is we thereby learn there are but a few basic requirements for our existence, happiness and well being. Chief among these is water. Bottles and bottles of the lovely stuff for drinking, gallons and gallons of the clear liquid for toileting, reservoirs and lakefuls of the ubiquitous substance for washing. The real importance of water, when it can truly be said to have come of age, comes when you see it getting the same cooled shelf space as Coca-Cola and Fanta in McDonalds outlet in Disneyland. The fact that Evian 75cl sports pack bottles were flying out over the counter at a faster rate than the coke infused liquid, tells its own story.

So we had done all our doings, seen all our seeings and were meandering our way through the lesser of out targeted exhibits when something bit at me inside my head and made me want to do the fatherly thing and take a few snaps of the children together before the background disappeared and their smiles wore off. I had managed to avoid this duty all day by entrusting the camera's carriage and use to each of the older children in turn by way of the fact that I had the cool-bag to carry. My reaction after I took the first picture brought the biggest laugh of he day, a laugh mixed with incredulity and a little of that oh, shitness. Yes, you've guessed it, there was no film in the camera. Who's a smart boy then?

Perhaps memories don't last as long as photographs; perhaps they can't be traded in smiles of one-upmanship with friends and relations; but hey, isn't that great?

The memories are there and theirs alone.

Chapter Four

French Heaven

French people are very polite, pedestrians say 'pardon' as they walk through you, drivers indicate as they attempt to drive over you. It's not that they mean you any harm, they don't, it's just that they have a different way of doing things because they have a different psyche. Space, that's the reason for the difference. We islanders from the cold north regard every square inch of space around our person as our own, in the same way as we lay claim to every square inch of water around our island. The French are a touchy feely lot who insist on pretend kisses on the cheeks, which is all very fine and dandy and acceptable with regards their women folk but when it comes to the men – yuk!

We did the Eiffel Tower this morning and we even managed to take photographs with a film in the camera. When I say 'did' I mean the perfunctory metro journey to get there and back and in between times we strode up six hundred and seventy-nine steps to the second stage of the structure and back down again. Restaurants, shops, telephones, internet, telescopes, even toilets with a tip dish, everything on the structure is based on one singular design which is to take your money. It is the French who are doing this so it is all beautifully done, on a wonderful scale, in the most magnificent of surroundings. This is no mere accident for the French didn't come upon being a proud people all of a sudden recently, they obviously have been so for quite a number of centuries. Neither good nor bad fortune has stood in the way of their civic pride and of continually adding to this in measured form throughout succeeding generations. Business is so good hereabouts it is understandable why the Yanks felt they had to get a piece of the action in this Europe place because with queues like these you can charge what you like.

We're off then, out of Paris and, eventually, back into French country side – it is amazing how much easier it is to find you way out of a city such as Paris than it is to find you way in – off down the Loire valley, not too great a distance to a town called Blois.

I have found my French heaven, although hopefully this is just the first part of such, it is Blois. It is situated around the centre of France and it remains just as God intended only manmade in a picture perfect way on not too grand a scale. Towns and cities on hillsides always do much better than those on the flat and level settings and with the Loire flowing sweetly as you go over any of its three bridges then the scene is set. What also sets the town apart is its stone. It is a beautiful hard stone, which can be worked like and wears like marble and yet has the tone and strength of purpose of granite. Its churches are magnificent, the chateau stands in proud testimony to a time when building such must have had its rewards as well as its costs for the people of the town. I'm sure very few subscribed joyfully to the notion of paying their hard earned dues to some prat in a poncy castle. By the same token I'm sure they were damn glad of the prat's poncy castle when unwanted strangers came a calling.

The whole town is a masterpiece of classical French building. I say building when meaning is in architecture because I'm sure there were not too many architects residing in the small towns of France between the thirteenth and eighteenth centuries when the majority of the buildings were completed. The builders and master craftsmen, by way of their paymasters were responsible for beautiful stone worked buildings seven and eight storeys high, with ornate features and wonderful roofs under which there were another couple of attic floors. The buildings are a proud testimony to and reflection of the growth in the fields of the countryside where everything stands tall and handsome and healthy. We in the desolate frozen northern region didn't have a land full of trees tall enough to give our beams and joists great reach, with very few exceptions – castles and round towers – we got stuck on the first floor. Richness in sun and soil meant the French could afford to pay the best craftsmen from countries all around to come and work on their projects and add to the skills already there. Alas, we on the periphery had and still have the option to go out and try to catch fish and get soaked for our trouble or go out and dig up some spuds and get a good drenching. Life is definitely a lot easier where the sun shines.

My children are getting closer to me, Caroline closer still, Rebecca closest of all. I'll deal with the last one first, the first one second and the second one last. Rebecca will not accept any advice when it comes to buying clobber for herself but most especially for her feet except that which emanates from teenage girlie magazines; with the result that she wears very stylish high heeled footwear. These are absolutely useless in their supposed primary function of being an aid to walking, in fact they are the exact opposite if the number of cuts and plasters on Rebecca's feet are anything to go by. Thus when it comes to going up or down even the slightest of inclines she needs a strong arm to attach herself onto in the practice of her stilt walking; my ears are still ringing with the torture she endured and thus passed on to me by way of her loquacious moaning during the rise and fall of the six hundred and seventy-nine steps of the Eiffel torture tower.

The eight of us are bonding in a very functional manner. We are squeezed together so much of the time we each have had to adapt very quickly to functioning as a unit of eight instead of eight distinct individuals. This is excellent as an exercise in social science and social skills because each one has very quickly adapted their survival techniques so if they see something they want in a shop they go for it on their own and yet at the same time functioning as a pack when they feel their ice-cream level dropping dangerously low. They are all being brilliant; I suppose it's all new and exciting to them and this is continually shining out of their eyes.

Caroline and I have had to become the great double act, she says and we both do. It is a mixture of Harry Houdini, except all the tricks are pulled out of my pocket in note form and Mary Poppins, except that as well as a handbag containing all, Caroline pulls all the rest of her tricks out of the wagen. It's a masterful feat of management skills, the only problem is we have to continue it for a fair bit yet.

This is definitely one quick fire way of getting to know your children just as it is one sure fire way of your children getting to meet the real you.

I still cannot get over the French back road network, it is so clinical; if you find you are not where you are meant to be – some people call it getting lost – simply work your way round in circuitous movement and soon you are where you want to be. By comparison back home we seem to work on the cobweb principle where everything emanates from the centre, new roads being added onto and off old roads in a very

haphazard fashion. Get lost and you do just that, you end up having to try to find your way out of a warren of little tribal networks which run and twist and turn leaving you a lot further away than you were when you began. If you aren't lost at the start of your locating efforts, you certainly are by the end of them.

Sitting out on a beautiful old terrace in Blois where undoubtedly tens of thousands have sat over the centuries watching the world go by, staring at the old town and at the same time enjoying a delicious dinner, life surely doesn't get much sweeter than this. It is sheer heaven on earth. Unless you are a six-year-old who finds the odd stray greenfly not very amusing and definitely not very appetising. Unless you are a nine-year-old who has to get sitting beside his mother which causes a ripple of a rumpus with the 'I was here first' brigade stirring into action. Unless you are one of the older ones whose meal must come without more toppings than with. Unless, unless, unless. They all have their little quirks or condolences which need addressing on a time scale which flows faster than whatever it is that is going on around them and which concerns them so deeply for such a short space of time.

This is how families learn to function properly; this is how the young members of the family learn; this is how the parents learn. As a dad the trick is to smile and enjoy it all, in the same way I am enjoying the olives in my meal, something which in life I had always refused to eat before. Now, somehow, the setting is right for change both on the plate as well as in my head.

The format that has worked itself out for us is up and at it before eight in the morning so we are out of the hotel by around nine. Whatever town we're in we then hit and, armed with baguettes, croissants, fruit and juice we are ready to take on the world with anything it can throw at us for the following three hours. This morning in the Chateau de Blois we had a one and a half-hour magic show followed by a tour of the chateau. Magic is magic whatever language it is presented in especially when you are dealing with a pack of cards, a length of rope and a fair bit of slapstick. A visit to a chateau is a visit to a chateau, there's not much more I can say on the subject except that the children are used visiting my mother but they would never think of running around her house the way they did here; then again, I think mother's carpets have a civilising effect on children in the way that tile, marble and stone floors provide the echoes which tell the children's feet to run faster and faster.

Lunch cannot taste any nicer than when eaten in a small, private, beautiful park in the middle of Blois, eating a pleasant mixture of baguette stuffed with banana, croissants and cooled cans of Orangina in the shade of trees that are hundreds of years old. The grandest of these trees had wire supports running off the main lower branches and up high to where they were staked into the main trunk. You have to really care to do something as enormous as this albeit on a small scale. It is the message which this gives out which is enormous.

If you as a society care enough to look after a couple of branches on an old tree then you as a society will not fail those less fortunate in human terms than yourself. When you do for others you increase the chances that they will not fail you, they might not actually do for you but at least you reduce the chances of them doing against you. I suppose too that doing is a lot easier when doors and windows are left open to let in a bit of breeze, but the bit of breeze that finds its way around here is a warm and embracing one which is more than welcoming. Good fortune may be something that happens upon people a lot easier in these parts than elsewhere but we should carry as many of their good ways back with us with the hope and expectation of any small improvement growing.

Travelling at speeds not much in excess of 50kph from Blois in a southerly direction toward Limoges is not very good for you. Getting off the beautiful back roads with their manicured fields of vine and sunflower, their tidy little towns of which many are beginning to show their age, was achieved with a mighty sense of relief as we got on to the motorway. Travelling at speeds quite a bit in excess of 130kph is very good for you especially when you have a big distance to travel in the shrieking heat.

Into Limoges, a city famed for its porcelain products. I hope the residents of Limoges get down on their knees every day and thank God for porcelain because we searched and searched and could find no other recommendation for visiting here. It has the look of having been a thriving industrial and commercial centre up to about thirty years ago but since then its fortunes have been in very definite decline. It's as if the gold rush is over but a lot of the locals are staying put in the hope that a new vein will be found. Limoges has a good basic layout and it is in an excellent setting but almost everything about the place is tatty, ill kempt, grotty.

Still, we managed to find too much to eat at a little family run kerbside restaurant and for the copious quantity of Orangina we enjoyed they presented us with two Orangina frisbees. Children are obviously quicker into the holiday frame of mind than we adults are because they immediately headed off looking for somewhere safer to throw them. There was not a sound of 'it's mine'. They were enthusiastically followed by their mother whilst I picked up the rear having had to remain behind slightly longer in order to pay the bill. A small restaurant with so few tables and chairs at their disposal, perhaps the frisbees were a good investment on their part because they freed the tables an awful lot sooner than otherwise could have been expected.

Down a treat the frisbees did go, or is it up first and then down a treat the frisbees did go. In the big square along side of which we had parked the wagen Caroline and Rebecca sat yakety – yaking by the untreated water of the 1960s fountain while the rest of us found our measure with the flight of the frisbee and frisbeed away a good half hour much to the bemusement of a sprinkling of passing locals.

Getting to sleep at night in these hotel rooms ain't easy, the rooms are so warm. The further south you go the more of a necessity air conditioning becomes. If you open a window for a light breath of air then, especially in the evening when you have a light on, you are providing an open invitation to every insect within a couple of miles radius to come and feast on your body in the small hours of the morning. Last night I had to spend twenty minutes standing on top of the bed with a pillow, one not to be used, squashing the little blighters against the ceiling where they had the decency to congregate in the light circle cast by the bedside lamp.

These insects are not as easily bored as we are. You can be watching whatever on the television and the insects won't show even the slightest interest on what is on or even in the brightness that emanates from the little box. In general televisions in bedrooms are for the lonely, lost and sad and are a terrible distraction to us poor normals. After channel hopping for a couple of minutes I settle back to absorb the misery that is EuroNews which, apart from the weather reports, its real attraction lies in the fact that there is something both absorbing and reassuring about other people's bad luck.

My two poor older boys keep having to go to their own room to use the bathroom, I think they must be suffering from that other television station which nobody ever watches.

We only thought we got up early. At every hotel so far breakfast has been served between six o'clock and nine-thirty in the morning. If this was tried back home I reckon there would be no breakfast eaten simply because there wouldn't be anyone to either prepare or serve out the food so early in the morning. When we enter these hotel car parks before ten o'clock at night they are full to the brim with cars and when we leave before nine o'clock in the morning the car parks are virtually empty; and someone mentioned these people are on holiday.

Chapter Five

Hills & Valleys

For the first Sunday in nine very long years I managed to take my family to Mass and it was in a grand although inornate church in a town called Brive. Unfortunately it was a special Mass for the local middle aged hysterical singers association who turned out in poor numbers to greet us in mediocre voice. They were manipulated by a master puppet mistress who stood on the first step of the altar as she jiggled and juggled their throats with gesticulations of her right arm. The Mass itself was a curious mixture. There was singing in French with the organ belching from on high; there was chanting in Latin; there was the normal liturgy of the Mass in French.

The church was as it must have been when built hundreds of years ago apart from the addition of electric light and a couple of speakers. There were no pews just very plain straight backed chairs with wicker seats, some of which had dulled brass plates on the back of them indicating the name of a local person shrewd enough to invest his or her money to good advantage. For old people especially, churches are a no lose gamble because first of all they can't take the money with them and anyway, if they are right and there is a big God waiting for us in the hereafter then they've won there too. There were no statues in the church, only very plain Stations of the Cross on the walls. Since there were no pews there was nothing to kneel on and therefore kneeling was not included in the solemnity of the occasion but there was an awful lot of standing.

Out and away from the old well-dressed dears in the church and on to the boulangerie for our bread sticks. We made the mistake first of all of going into what we took to be a bread shop but the lady serving looked down her nose at us as she pointed us on up the street explaining that she was a patisserie. A second glance around the shop confirmed she was selling an absolutely delicious selection of delectable delights but it was bread that we needed for now.

Armed with baguettes and fluids we headed into the park where, beside a fountain and some very modern sculptures we munched our plain brunch. There were plenty of pigeons around and the youngest three children immediately acquired the knack of feeding the birds little bits of their bread whilst scaring them away at the same time. There are a great number of double lined trees of enormous proportion angled out to the periphery of the park from this central area and the bark of these trees is a wonderful display of camouflage colours. Some bright spark decided there was no need for lamp-posts here so instead electric cables run up every third or forth tree to spotlights that shine down from on high.

Onward through the splendid Dordoyne region which is a continuation of first class arable land with forests up over the hillsides and through the valleys. Our next stop hotel is in a quaint little town called Labastide Murat where we were ensconced in the three rooms at the top of the house. The house is in fact a thirteenth century mansion right in the centre of the village and it is every bit my idea of what a hotel should be. Architecturally and structurally it is magnificent; seated

terraces both front and rear it has only twenty bedrooms each of which has been fitted out to the 'nth' degree which includes everything from first class ensuite, to air conditioning; you name it, it has it. As you exit your bedroom the landing lights have been taught such good manners that they automatically come on. It is the quality of the fixtures and fittings, which most impresses. This is definitely a cut above any of the hotels we previously stayed in.

The girls have a room, the boys have a room, Caroline and myself have a room, it's a simple, straightforward set up. Except when the other two rooms are regarded as hallowed ground by their occupants and squeals of horror follow even a sighting of one of the other species in close proximity to their revered door. Hilarious! Almost as funny as Caroline's reaction the other morning when she realised something had been stolen from our car. My reaction was my normal couldn't care less, the engine and steering wheel were still intact so I was happy enough. It was the country demarcation sticker that was stolen off the back of the wagen and Caroline's horror was due to the fact that we could now be mistaken for a race of people that we weren't.

A long, long walk in glorious sunshine is something we have not had a lot of experience of this or any recent summer for that matter. Absolutely brilliant then as the eight of us strolled casually through French countryside listening to crickets cricketing in the fields, the children happy because they had themselves convinced that a shop selling ice-pops and ice-creams was just around the next corner or the next or the next. It didn't matter to me if there was or there wasn't; if there was so well and so good we would all then have religiously pleasurable ice-cream to pep us up for the return journey; if there wasn't, so what, we had to make our way back no matter what. The walk back to the hotel didn't quite have the same zipidee doodah for the children so the girls drew in a close pack to discuss all the shops they were going to attack with their purses when next we reached proper civilisation and the boys headed off butterflying. They haven't quite got the measure of French butterflies though for they didn't manage to catch a single one between them.

On our return journey we slowed again to watch the communal playtime exertions of the locality at their fenced off outdoor swimming pool situated near a crossroads in the middle of nowhere. It would have been bad manners to stand and stare no matter how much the boys may have wanted to; their fun seems so much more normal and relaxed because it's in the great outdoors when compared to our noisy, smelly indoor swimming pools at home.

Back from the enormous exertions of our sunny time walking and after freshening up we headed off in the wagen to find a shop of any sort that sold the lemonades, ice-pops and ice-creams, so longed for by the children. Not a bit of it. We must have driven for well over thirty miles but there was nothing open, it was a Sunday and the French do not waken on a Sunday at all. We were very glad that we had already made a booking in the hotel's La Garissade restaurant for a dinner to remember. A gastronomic experience to be remembered is how they advertised it.

Were they ever right!

Everything about the meal was delicious, probably. I savoured glasses of locally produced grape juice and apple juice. The starter was a mixed blessing of fruits and vegetables finely cut and beautifully stacked in a torrine shape and with a bitey sauce. Main course for most was lamb along with the usual vegetables but the lambs out here must have a really easy life they had so much fat on them. Dessert was a challenge as much for your plate as for your belly. The problem was you were allowed to take what you wanted from about twenty different dessert dishes the like of which you would not see in your fanciest restaurant at home. It would not have mattered how big your dish was and, believe me, it was big, you would not have enough room to satisfy your greed. The smart ones I noticed, filled their dishes once but ended up the evening with two dessert dishes each in front of them.

I can think of only one word to best describe the whole eating experience – tart. In their menu they state that not only do they take great pride in the food they prepare and cook but that their suppliers also take great pride in the quality of food they produce. The complete eating experience was certainly different, certainly entertaining, certainly a world away in terms of taste buds from the sweetened, processed, bulked up, sauced, tasteless tripe we are served up in most hostelries at home. Our taste buds probably weren't ready for the experience but my oh my it certainly revitalised them to the extent that they are never going to forget it in a hurry.

Amusement for the evening was provided by a troupe of flies. It was evident from their manner they had trained long and hard in their chosen profession and they had their restaurant routine off to a 't'. They had us swinging and swiping with our arms, they had us ducking and cursing as we took centre stage in their evening finale, to the enormous amusement of the local diners gathered at tables around us. So well mannered and well trained were the fly troupe in La Garissade restaurant they would not eat a bite of food off your or anyone else's plate, they preferred instead to eat off your fork. During the course of the entertainment the only complaining that we could see was by the flies about the eating habits of some of the other guests, their table manners were so poor the flies would not trouble them for a bite to eat. In that none of the other diners came over all wavy and slammy it was more than obvious we were the special guests of the evening.

Chapter Six

Getting Hot

I have decided that between now and Marbella I am going to change the habits of a lifetime; I am going to buy a pair of swimming trunks. The last time I wore a pair of swimming trunks while standing in anger looking at a body of water was almost thirty years ago. Then, as now, I had absolutely no interest in this area of divestment either in a posing or using fashion. Now, unlike then, I feel I'll need a pair of trendy trunks to join with the rest of the family in jumping into a body of cooling water. The further south we go and the greater the temperature the greater the appeal of lying docile in a cool clear pool. If thirty odd degrees provides a sweat bubbling experience, what on earth is forty odd degrees going to provide – sweat boiling?

Monday it is and it turned out not to be too great a day. It's not that there was too much travelling, not a bit of it; too little rehydration early on led me to lose my cool for the first time. We left Labastide Murat in the morning and we headed off to Cahors. Cahors was beautiful early on in the day as we loped about enjoying a lazy brunch but even this early in the day it was hot hot hot. This, the southern region of France, has heat in abundance; it's just that today they were overdoing it a bit. Cahors has a mental angle on heat with its wonderful fountain displays at almost every turn which is great because this feeling and presence of water in voluminous form has a positive effect on the psyche. They must be real magnets for pulling shoppers in from the surrounding heat but not today, there were very few about. There was only one boulangerie open in the centre of town and here we bought our staple diet of breads along with cans of apple and orange juice. Could we find anywhere that sold bottles of water? Not a chance. We thought they must be a real lazy bunch hereabouts because apart from a few bars that were open everything else in town remained firmly shut.

On to Montauban, a journey of only an hour or so down the road. We parked at the side of a respectable looking church, which had four of the most enormous statues out its front. Walkabout then for a while led Caroline and the girls into a trendy air-conditioned ladies clothes shop wherein they quickly disappeared. Myself and the boys walked aimlessly up and down and around in the soaring heat of early afternoon, the boys had their hat and caps on, I had my 'Indiana Jones' style hat on which I had bought in Blois. There was not one other shop open in the immediate vicinity so we walked round in a square to try not to get lost, keeping to the shaded side whenever possible. The heat by this stage was killing especially since we hadn't had anything to drink in over an hour and our intake had been poor before that.

Finally, after wandering up and down outside the shop I sent word into Caroline that we were going. The look on her face when she and the girls came out shortly after blew my gasket and it took me a while longer than usual to put my lid back on. I know it was a tad unfair of me to call them out before they had managed to actually purchase anything, that is assuming they were ever going to get around to buying something. They knew there were few if any other such shops open and it had been a few days since they had been able to indulge themselves in a good session of retail therapy so they went for it, obviously knowing that it could be as long again before they got the chance of another dose of it.

Hip, hip hooray for McDonald's, they saved the day. I'm coming round to appreciating McDonald's more and more, especially now I've discovered their McFlurry range of ice creams with bits of whatever type of sweet broken and mixed in for good measure, Dime is a real delight. The only criticism I can make of it is there is too much of it to enjoy, or perhaps my stomach has shrunk down to French portion size instead of our American portion sizes back home.

Take a tip from me, you know by now I'm an old hand at this holiday lark, don't book into hotels in big shitties or even cities such as Toulouse where we have arrived for our last stop in France. Make sure it is definitely not in the suburbs because it's a pig to find; make sure it is positively not in the flight path of the nearby airport because you'll find it difficult to get to sleep plus I don't believe them about their loos; make sure it is absolutely not during a thunderstorm. Also, when you are this far south and so far inland, make sure the little room with the bed has air conditioning. With all the aforementioned points in mind we

decided that early to bed was the best option since we had already eaten and since we did not want to go out anywhere this evening simply because we might never find the hotel again. Early to bed would also give us the chance of rising before the crack of dawn and thus having a good go at Spain's motorways tomorrow. The children were all in agreement with this, they had had a tough day and there was nothing of interest to them around here.

The best laid plans and all that...

I have a bit of an idea of what it must have been like for the residents of Dresden and Coventry, and other such cities that essentially suffered carpet bombing during World War Two. The thunder sounded for all the world like bombing in the near distance and, since there was a tall hedge about ten metres from our ground floor windows, all that could be seen above the hedge was a pinky red brilliance of light. What a thunder and lightning show, it took it a couple of hours to calm down but for all its huffing and puffing there wasn't a drop of water.

I awoke around three in the morning after about three hours broken sleep; after about a ten second consultation with Caroline we decided to go for it. We got everyone shifted, washed, toothed, dressed, packed, teed, bags and suitcases out weighing my arms down as I carried them out to the wagen and PWAH! Some delinquent had smashed the driver's door window to break into the wagen. The dirty lowlife scum took the bag containing all of Caroline's clothes, the bag containing sun lotions and other such products as well as maps and books, they picked through the rest of the family clothes stealing only new and nearly new clothes as well as shoes and, wait for it, the big bag containing all our dirty washing for the journey so far.

Caroline and some of the children had appeared by now. For a split second you stand there gawking at each other wondering what you have done to deserve this. It's three thirty in the morning, you're in a shit hole of a place on the outskirts of a dirty big city, the airport down the road hasn't stopped all night and now this. You stand outside yourself wondering what to do but this only lasts for a couple of seconds. It is dead simple; you clear as much of the broken glass out of the wagen with your metal ice scraper, then load everyone and everything on board and get OTF.

One of the problems is that this is obviously a short stay stopover hotel which is empty of personnel after early evening, there isn't even a night porter on duty, the majority of its clientele are probably airport users. The most important thing this hotel has is a sign at its entrance declaring the car park to be 'Non Garder'. In my book that's an open invitation to thieves. Anyway, stuff phoning the police and waiting God knows how long for them to arrive – a police report is necessary for insurance purposes but how many days is that going to take? – Stuff waiting for three or four hours or more for a member of the hotel staff to appear. As soon as I checked the extra stash of cash was safely deposited where I had taped it before we left home I could breathe again and so we were off.

Chapter Seven

Spain in a Day

I have long held an inkling that some day I'd like to take Caroline in a classic car and for the three of us to do a nice run from Paris to Monte Carlo and back. If the car is up to it I'll do it in my sleep because today, with the prior agreement of all concerned – the truth is none of us had a clue what we were letting ourselves in for – we drove, minus one window, from about ten miles north of Toulouse down to Marbella on the very southern tip of Spain. It was a sixteen hour solid drive, give or take an hour, with three pit stops in petrol stations to refuel and defuel.

It was the wacky races. I grabbed the steering wheel with both hands in the supposedly correct 'ten to two' position and I held on for grim death. I sank my right foot deep into the accelerator pedal and tried not

to travel at under ninety miles per hour. Concentration was total, for the complete journey my two eyes scanned the road ahead, the traffic behind, sign posts, maps, everything visual was absorbed and acted upon and we got away with it, almost. I had forgotten the number one rule in distance anything – relax. For three days after I had a headache and the morning after I threw up. Yes. A small price to pay and thoroughly deserved.

Spain's biggest problem is the fact that its near neighbour is France and this is the level on which it is going to be judged and compared. Unfortunately, petrol stations in Spain do not stand up well when compared with their French cousins. In our first stop, which was not a great distance into Spain the bathroom facilities were useable but the food was distinctly lacking and as we progressed the level of hygiene at service stations diminished.

France is sublime. Spain is arid. Spain does very well then considering what it has to work with which is a dry baked basin where they have to work hard at every bit of scrub between and often on the sides of the mountains. I have only seen the Mediterranean coast so far and this was a high speed, so what would I know? The way I was feeling when I was driving it – what did I care either?

With this crazy piece of driving it meant we would be at the apartment in Spain a day or two early, that is if we could ever find it. Our maps detailing the difficult directions to the apartment were among those stolen and with the maps it was never going to be easy to find. I phoned back home and Ciaran told me Mary and her daughter Katie were still there, what a stroke of luck. In the end up a phone call to Mary meant she came out and found us and we were then able to follow her back to the apartment. The following morning as Mary headed for the airport and when I made it out of the bathroom we headed off into Fuengirola, which housed the nearest Volkswagen dealer. Fortunately also, Mary was able to leave Caroline a lot of her clothes and bits and pieces to keep her going until she got herself sorted.

We arrived at the garage in the early afternoon, it was closed for siesta. It opened again from five until nine in the evening so, after another couple of hours lie down, we headed off and yippedy doodle they were open. No luck though as this was a Volkswagen car dealership and our Caravelle is classed as a van and the nearest van centre is a distance away in Malaga. No problem. Off to Malaga we trot and after a couple of hours searching, which included a visit to the tourist office for directions, we finally found it. With the eight of us not having one word of Spanish between us I gesticulated in all manner of meaning to the poor salesman in the showroom who hadn't a word of English.

"Si. Si." Words of great truth and meaning, and brevity, finally issued from his bemused face, at last we were in business. Oh no we weren't. He lifted a sheet of paper and drew us out a short map of where we needed to go. It was less than half a mile away. Half a mile away is good if you are walking; half a mile away is better if it is in the direction which traffic is travelling; half a mile away is no good when you are headed the wrong way in a one way traffic system in a big city. After breaking only a couple of traffic regulations we finally got there. It was ten minutes to nine. The place closed at eight thirty.

I am not saying it is all their fault, I am not saying it is partly their fault, what I am saying is that the lack of road signs in southern Spain borders on the phenomenal. Advertising in every shape and form and advertising everything under the sun is everywhere; big billboards, small ones; at the side of roads, up hillsides; but try to get a sign that tells you where you are not to mention one that will tell you where you want to get to, forget it.

We made it back into the apartment at around ten at night, worn out, starving, headache, absolutely knackered and mission incomplete. Fortunately, Caroline still held a bit of something in reserve and did her mother hen bit and rallied us so that while I sat with the boys watching a DVD of Gladiator, out came delicious platefuls of taglietelle whatever with oven chips thrown on top for good measure, and God knows what tasty morsels for the children.

Spain in a day, I thoroughly recommend it. If you can do it any quicker I recommend that too. On the motorway down we passed lorry after lorry after lorry after lorry after lorry after lorry ad infinitum. Where were they all going? South obviously, but why? It is a long coastline, there must be numerous ports; there is a railway line, we saw plenty of train activity.

It was only when we scaled the last of our mountains on the way down and followed the coast road that we saw the scale of the problem. It is a concrete jungle on a scale the Amazon forest would have been proud of in its heyday. Along the length of the coastline for as far as the eye can see there is nothing but tall concrete monuments to people's hope of rescue from their misery. Half the uncivilised world seems to have been drawn here by the reality of uninterrupted sunshine. It is on a scale that my eyes could hardly believe and my mind did not want to absorb. Cranes were swinging slowly everywhere spreading the rash higher and higher up the hills, further and further along the coast. I never thought I could dislike anything so much and I suppose it provides some form of welcome release for many, not for me though, it was making me shudder and this was from afar.

When we got down into it it was full of all that holds a special abhorrence for me. Cheap, nasty little bars, restaurants and clubs that offer the basest forms of self indulgence to the vast populace and here the emphasis is on vast because every street, path and corner thronged with those on a mission to love themselves as much as they could manage while they pretend to be their favourite film or pop star. This is where they get to play at being who they are not but who they see themselves as being. This is where for two weeks every year they leave the ugly frog behind them in some grotty suburb in England, Germany, France or wherever and coax the prince or princess in them out with a bottle of factor whatever in one hand and a bottle of Sangrilla in the other.

Okay, we get too much rain at home but does that mean as soon as they step off a plane they leave their sense of reason behind? Of course not. There is a growing number of every strata of society that will perform to the basest of standards that they can, when they can. They act the same at home on their blistered nights out, the only difference is that out here they get to do it day in day out, night in night out, and without much in the line of clothes on.

Enough of my moaning, this is their place in the sun not mine and they are more than welcome to their piece of it.

Oh yes, we made it back into Malaga the following morning and got the window fixed in an Auto Glass workshop, Volkswagen vans didn't do them but we'll not go into the detail of it.

Chapter Eight

Settling In

The children have settled into a nice routine of breakfast, pool, lunch, pool, dinner, pool, shop, pool, dvd, and bed. Caroline is waiting for word back from the holiday company for a change of dates so I can get back to my drizzly climate between seven and ten days earlier than arranged. I know I shouldn't change plans as a reaction to what has happened but I did honestly feel beforehand that a full month spent in Spain was a bit too much. I don't think I'm quite ready for that yet. I discussed it with Caroline and the children, in my own inimitable fashion, and all are in agreement. At the moment we're waiting for a phone call back and making plans to go to somewhere called Puerto Banus this afternoon to take care of a lot of shopping Caroline needs to make up in some measure for what was stolen.

The phone call came and confirmed we are now heading back out of Cherbourg on the 21st August at six o'clock in the evening, this takes ten days off our stay and we now just need to reschedule the six nights going back up through France. I don't think Toulouse will be one of our stops. I feel greatly relieved, I can manage what is before me now. I think Caroline is relieved too, probably as much for my sake as for returning early enough to sort out new school uniforms for the children. The children also prefer the idea of going back and having time in the streets and up and around the town with their friends instead of going straight back into school.

The nicest thing about eating lunch al fresco is coming back inside and watching the tiny birds pecking up after us. The not nicest thing about eating lunch al fresco is the flies. The really nice thing about eating lunch al fresco is eating lunch. I think it must be eating not to a set time but to need. We have certainly cut back big time on the amounts we consume at home; here it is on a need to eat basis whereas at home it is almost as if it is on a volume uncontrol basis. We seem to be learning, perhaps the heat is helping, in a perfidious way.

Today we went shopping. Ola. I think today is Friday; it doesn't feel

like Friday but it doesn't matter a jot what day it is. We went to Puerto Banus, it is a very pleasant little coastal town where the streets are not thronged with people, where the shops are very tellingly more upmarket and where you get the feeling that there is space and air to breathe and life is at a bit more leisurely pace. Perhaps I can think and breathe properly because half of our problem has been solved and we expect a phone call around six-thirty this evening to confirm the other half has been solved too. I hope and trust we will be telephoned with suitable arrangements.

It was amiss of me to think I could stand nearly a full month of glorious sunshine in a great apartment here somewhere in the Costa del Sol with my wife and six. The old self isn't that easily disposed of; it has been a long time in the making and to think that a few days and one or two thousand miles distance could leave it behind was hopeful to say the least and downright stupid to tell the truth. Here I am a week and a half into this supposed change of bearing if not of being, we've had some highs, we've had some lows and since Toulouse we've had a skinful of stress thrown in which is exactly the opposite of the purpose of the holiday. The new man might well be lurking somewhere within me but it is going to take a hell of a lot of relaxation and sunshine to melt away the old exterior.

An old pal I used to teach under, who was also a friend of my father's in their youth – Michael Quigley – when told recently that I was going away on a long holiday with my family, said:

"Liam, holiday? Sure Liam wouldn't be interested in a holiday unless there's a challenge in it for him!"

I am probably not on my own here. I'd say a lot of us men, fathers, husbands, sons, brothers, uncles, or whatever we pass for as beings, are totally misunderstanding of our selves, our selfhood and generally the predicament we find ourselves in in life. Life is changing with each decade and we have to learn to change with it.

I know I needed a break not just from the past in terms of work but also the past in terms of the person I had worked myself into being, this self that I had become for whatever number of reasons. As Tom, the brother says:

"Now we're both in our forties, we have to learn to do things the lazy way!"

It goes against the grain to even think that way not to mention act that way when from no age at all we were taught to work hard and to waste nothing. Time was not to be wasted, money certainly wasn't to be wasted.

Understanding appreciates with age as almost everything else about the person deteriorates.

Our work ethic as with most else in life was drilled into us by mother. A mother who is and always has been a golfer, a good one in terms of winning a lot throughout her years and regularly so still; golf is something I would put into the waste of time category. Whereas before I would have wasted seventy pence or so on a newspaper not for the little bits of news, information or gossip that it bought but I regarded it a good investment because there might also be something of commercial use or value to me. It is only now I am beginning to understand that the seventy pence is an investment in my self, in the time I take away from the battling of my world in order to peruse the thoughts and inklings of others. It is taking some time out and devoting it to yourself, that inner being so long lost inside your outer shell.

Ah, the telephone call from the holiday company came, everything is sorted, rearrangements have been made for the return journey which is due to begin on or around the thirteenth, a probable couple of nights in Spain, followed by six nights up through France, followed by the boat from Cherbourg on the twenty-first, followed by the road home.

    A delicious meal was prepared and cooked by Caroline and myself in the tidy kitchen, served by Caroline and Rebecca and enjoyed by all. In our kitchen at home the whole family can stand and sit and work around each other without much banging into anyone or pushing or squeezing; out here if three are gathered together in the kitchen then the fridge door cannot be opened – but it works, it is brilliant, so little space and so many gathered together is great. We must be on holiday, at last. Dessert was a nestling of the family together in the lounge area where we laughed away the ills of the past few days with the help of Eddie Murphy in a dvd of Dr. Dolittle 2, not bought for any real reason other than the fact it was the one good film in the buy one get one free section. Laughter certainly is the best tonic. The other film we acquired, obviously the get one free one, "El Mensajero Del Miedo' yeah, that was my first reaction too but it turns out you can watch it (listen to it?) in any of five different languages or in subtitle form for a further twelve languages. It is an old film, about forty years of age, starring Frank Sinatra, Lawrence Harvey, and Jane Leigh and its real name is 'The Manchurian Candidate'. The older children are at the stage now where what they watch is extremely important to them, it is obviously some sort of stain on their character if they are made to watch something they are not interested in. It used to be enough for them and it still is enough for the younger ones to get sitting up late, eating sweets and chocolate.

    This morning, I think it is Saturday but I couldn't swear on it, is the first morning since our arrival in Spain that I rose with a clear head, the headache has gone. It is a real luxury being able to go to bed at whatever time suits and get up in the morning at whatever time your body clock tells you to. It is strange therefore that we are in bed before midnight every night and up before nine o'clock every morning. When we were at home in the old mould it was impossible to bring yourself to get into bed before midnight any night not to talk of the nights prior to having to get up at six in the morning. Which begs the question: what do all these lost hours of sleep do to your mind, your psyche, your sense of balance in life, not to mention your behaviour with the rest of your family? A question perhaps best left unanswered.

This morning then, I chased the rest of the family off to the swimming pool – it didn't take much chasing – telling them I would clear up and do the breakfast dishes. I honestly cannot remember when I last washed and dried, put away and tidied up after a meal, apart from maybe a small one, myself. Of course I have futtered, I have helped out, I have rinsed out, I have even dried dishes. The space inside my head that was cleared by performing these simple actions and functions in the kitchen was enormous. Nor was the enormity of this lost on the faces or in the heads of the children. It was obviously a whole new meaningful experience for them for daddy to stay behind in the kitchen in the morning while they headed out the door. Experiences like this last long in the consciousness of children and can have a wonderful telling effect on their development so long as they understand this change is real and not something temporary. The change of the course of the plough must be true as well as permanent.

Today, as yesterday, as tomorrow, there are no clouds in the sky; sometimes we have this at home too when the sky is a complete grey and the days are dark and dreary; here the sky is blue, the sun is shining even though it is early on in the day. There is a haze, which runs what appears to be the whole length of the coastline, it even comes down to rest upon some of the taller of the hotel and apartment buildings. I suspect the haze lifts with the sleepiness and tiredness of the holidaymakers as they make their escape from beds around midday.

When I was young holidays, as with life in general, seemed plagued by a lack of readies in my pocket. On the basis of this I have decided to play a game with the children for their amusement as much as for my own. When we go into a shop to buy even an ice cream whichever one of them happens to be closest to me at the time gets the change. I have added to this the past few days, although I don't anticipate it happening too often, by asking whenever one of the younger ones is crying after being hurt or when one of the older ones looks a bit down, how many Euro they need to make them better. It is peculiar how the amount always matches a handy note size.

It is therapy of a kind that might teach them something about themselves, about others, about me and the way they should be, and about money. In any case I would otherwise be handing them out the same money to go to the local shop for the chewy and fizzy sweet delights they consider worth so many visits to their dentist's chair. By now Thomas and Peter each have around thirty to forty percent more money than they began the holiday with. Rebecca, with regular topping up on my part and God knows how much from her mother, has touched base twice so far and currently stands at forty percent of what she started with. It provides a good insight into all of our natures.

I am beginning to understand how people can get into this life of sitting around in good weather only doing the things that please you, which for most of them doesn't seem to amount to very much. For all I know relaxing might even be good for you, just so long as like everything else in life you learn to keep a proper balance between what you should do and what you need to do. Fine words indeed coming from an eejit like myself whose last holiday was honeymoon seventeen years ago and who is about as relaxed as a tightly wound spring coil could be. I am learning, I hope.

By the way, I have only just discovered that Caroline, my wife of many a short cool summer, is a private beach bum. This has probably come as a great surprise to herself too as it has been a long time since the sun has even looked at her not to talk of paint her outer layer brown. Private here means our patio and back garden areas as opposed to the very public displays of fat so many of the holidaymakers make by lying about as naked as public health restrictions allow, basking in their fortnight of nothingness except sunshine.

I have also discovered that I hadn't quite grasped the full extent of communal living. There are noises now coming from next door and their speciality is the sound of a baby crying at night-time. This is a nuisance, it is not a problem. Every apartment has its designated car parking space and we have yet to be able to get into ours, an Audi owner from Belgium has determined it to be his, he is welcome to it. They couldn't have picked a space further away from the apartment if they had tried and there are plenty of free spaces over where it makes sense for us to park. This is not a problem, it is a solution to a nuisance. However, wandering out of the apartment onto the patio and sauntering

on into the garden area and finding that you are six or seven feet away from a couple of over friendly, over sized and over the fence type of foreign neighbours in razzle-dazzle bathing suits makes me come over all cold and want to put some clothes on to protect myself, but normally I beat a hasty retreat back indoors. This is not a problem, this is a nuisance being himself.

We made it back into Puerto Banus today. Caroline, having enjoyed it so much yesterday but feeling that now she had found her feet, so to speak, she could make a better showing of herself in some of the shops. First port of call had to be the port, well it would, wouldn't it? Holy Macaroni! We have all heard of the idle rich, we may even have encountered one or two of them in passing from time to time. If you want to find where they hide out look no further than Puerto Banus. This is obviously one of their little playgrounds, one of their ports of call as they amuse themselves during their summer jaunts around the Mediterranean. Around the port are parked not the ordinary Mercedes and Porsches we see at home, they are specials and sports versions and convertibles and with them too there is a liberal sprinkling of Aston

Martins, Rolls Royces and every young boy's dream, the irrepressible Ferraris. Yipidedoohah cars all around.

In terms of cost, the cars were a mere trifle when it came to the boats. Unlike the cars, the boats held no desire for me; in my mind they smack of trouble, of something else that needs looking after; that needs plenty of time, space, money and ocean to be enjoyed fully. Then again I suppose the owners aren't the ones who are going to be getting up on top with the deck scrubber to do the necessary. The boats started off the size of a large van and as we walked along the shop and restaurant fronts, our heads at ninety degree angles to the rest of our bodies, the boats grew bigger and bigger until we ended up staring at ones larger than most two storey houses. Puerto Banus, one of the small dots on the map of the southern coastline of Spain, is filled with the idle rich; as opposed to most of the rest of the coastline which is over brimming with the idle not so rich.

I keep thinking of and feeling for the local Spaniards who have had all this foreign depravity thrust upon them since the mid 1960s. I'm sure many have found it very much to their liking because economically and commercially they are in a win win win situation. I'm just as sure many have found it to their dislike for what was once a part of Spain is now a multi-uncultured crust running the length of their Mediterranean coastline. I'm sure most have by now accepted that this is the way things not only are but are going to be with probably a majority of citizens having grown up with it as well as in it and therefore accept it for what it is – an opportunity with mixed blessings. It doesn't matter what you want the opportunity to be, suffice it to say there is any amount of opportunity for those who want to be good, bad, indifferent or different.

There is a little newsagents cum nik-nak shop just past the entrance gates to the marina area and beyond in Puerto Banus and in it I could not find a single Spanish newspaper for sale – I have sold newspapers these past nine years and I know this does not mean they were all sold – every English broadsheet and tabloid newspaper was for sale as were German, Dutch and other European papers, there were even American and Irish newspapers for sale. This is a true and obvious reflection of those who use the port. Now that I think of it, as we were leaving the marina area an enormous low loader with two medium sized boats, as its cargo, had to be carefully guided in by the guard on duty at the gates. I bet you this is how the vast majority of the boats have found their mooring; I'd say there's not one of these wouldn't be sailors has had a damp sock in years.

I really love having the time to help prepare the dinner. With time comes inclination. Standing barefoot on a marble floor, chopping peppers, mushrooms, garlic, strange shaped onions that do not seem to have one quarter of the acid content the ones at home have, is pure sweetness. Relaxation comes in the form of performing the supposedly menial tasks which are in reality the real and meaningful duties at home; seeing the expressions of joy on six young faces when they are handed out dinner which they not only adore but which you have had a hand in making, is priceless. Getting some of the younger ones to actually hand back a clean plate can sometimes require right and proper bribing of the afterwards:

"No sweets tonight unless I see clean plates."

They know what I mean.

Chapter Nine

Getting to Know

Sitting here staring out at green and distant leaves breathing gently in the breeze, I find it curious how man has very little bother creating transient happiness for himself no matter where he is or in what situation he finds himself. It is obviously just a quirk built in to help facilitate survival in whatever predicament we find ourselves caught up in. The highlight of the day today, apart from meal times, was going around the supermarket checking out all the strange local delights and amazing prices. Prices in Spain are at least twenty to thirty per cent lower than at home, which is what I regard as a competitive pricing policy.

Back to basics is what life out here essentially amounts to. For some people this amounts to eating, drinking, sleeping and doing very little else apart from the obvious, if they have it in them to do. Sorry, I nearly

forgot and using their mobile phones. Yes, they wander down to the pool, they pose around at the pool, and they lie around the pool, all the time with their little electronic obsessions stuck to the side of their face. The first company that launches a waterproof mobile phone is onto a sure fire winner because the more public a display these plonkers can make of themselves massaging their ego the better. I know I should not waste my time not to mention yours even talking about such persons but these are the same mentalities who use the patio and garden areas of their apartment to lie out sunning themselves in topless form. This I do not mind, it is quite acceptable, but for some women this is not enough, they insist on lying out completely naked and worse still, going down to the swimming pool to do this as well.

Exhibitionists they are trying to be and the sun is merely an excuse for them to divulge their fatty secrets. Laws are what are needed to protect most of us who have no desire to see other people's funny bits. There are some rules in place for the apartments but these need to be strengthened and enforced; for instance, at the moment dogs of the four-legged variety are not allowed near the pool, this rule could be extended to include the two-legged ones. Maybe I'm becoming an early old fuddy duddy, I don't think so, I prefer to think of myself as more of a purist; Caroline mentioned them but more in disgust at the shapes of the bodies on show; Rebecca did mind, she was truly disgusted; the twins Sarah and Emma were enthralled; the three boys were mad for it, out on the hunt at every given opportunity.

We'll have to go searching today to see if there is even a small bit of old Spain left around here. I reckon if we go inland we're bound to run into some form of civilisation eventually; we are not looking for bullrings or any of that playing to the gallery nonsense. It is supposedly Sunday and Caroline claims to be determined we all reaffirm our religious beliefs by finding a church and enjoying a Sunday service. This is going to be difficult. I can honestly say I have not seen one chapel, church, synagogue, mosque, temple or whatever blend of building you wish to invest your faith in, along the whole length of the Spanish Mediterranean coast. They must be hereabouts somewhere, it's just that they are no longer as visible as they once were due to the new towering monuments to self escapism; the fact that I have to drive so fast probably hasn't helped much either.

In France the difficulty was in missing them. French towns and cities have retained their original core and building out from this has been done in as sympathetic a fashion as differing times through the various centuries have allowed. Unlike a lot of the countryside at home the French countryside remains much as it must have been in Napoleon Bonaparte's dying years. My smattering of French history indicates the reason for this as French inheritance law, which insists the eldest son inherits the farm. In the centuries and decades gone by this was obviously good for the professions, for the colonies, for the Church, for business and trade as well as for the towns and cities; it was also very good news for the countryside. What this guards against is the sub-division of the countryside, which leads to unmanageably small lots because before long you find that you are into the sub-division of the sub-divisions.

Anyway, we have to find a church, not by way of any religious fervour, ours is more an uncomplaining type of religion – if we don't bother it it shouldn't bother us – rather, more along the lines of the motor car. It's like a weekly fill up; you fill your tank at the start of the week and, with any luck, this should see you through to the following Sunday. There's no point in taking unnecessary risks now is there?

Right, that's it. I've finally done it. No, we didn't manage to get to church, we couldn't find a church or some reason like that will have to do you. No, what I mean is that I finally bought The Sunday Times, no, not the business just a copy of The Sunday Times. More to the point I actually read through all of it on a Sunday afternoon. Firstly, I cannot remember when I last bought one of these massive word collections – I have long felt that I would be cheating my descendants out of their heritage of appalling weather by way of doing a stocky little Brazilian rain forest dweller out of his home – my Sunday was never long enough for one of these papers. Secondly, I cannot remember when I ever read it and here I must qualify by explaining that 'reading' actually means absorbing the sections of the sections that claim some short interest to my eyes.

What this newspaper has done is help me relax by whiling away a couple of hours shaded from the sun while the rest of the family did

whatever it is people do at or around swimming pools or on sun loungers while leggering themselves with the contents of factor whatever. Right before my eyes, in amazement during the space of a very few days Caroline has transmogrified herself from a hard working, no nonsense, all business self at home to this jelly shape in recliner mould trying to make her outer layer of skin look as though she overdosed on HP sauce.

    I cannot say I am very taken with this lazing on a Sunday afternoon bit at all; I would much rather walk the couple of miles to our excellent Fiorentini's ice cream parlour at home and then walk on to visit a friend or relation on the way back, than stagnate in a chair with nothing better to do than absorb the mental warblings of others. A friendly bit of social discourse is much more to my liking than this packaged pretence aid for Sunday survival. The biggest surprise I had in reading The Sunday Times is how little news there actually is in it, its main preoccupation seems to be to annoy and worry rather than inform and answer. Anyway, my life is too short for spending even the slightest bit of it absorbing other people's crap.

The idea of finding a church just because it was Sunday – isn't every day sun day on the Costa del Sol? – died a very quick and sudden death when I said: 'Sure go you all to the pool'. That was all the encouragement they needed since the whole lot of them have taken to this swimming nonsense with great aplomb. They are away back to the pool again after dinner. Stephen being the first one out because this afternoon we took a quick run into Belamodena for him to get one of those inflatable boats. He chose it himself of course and he has been busting a gut since to get using it. Off to the pool he shot but before he could say: 'I name this ship...' some old woman – not the exact words Stephen used to describe her – squawked at him: "No boats! No boats!"

His tears were soaking the patio as he stood, his big head disconsolately hung low, his boat tucked dryly under his right arm. "We'll soon see about that!" thundered from his mother's heart as she grabbed Stephen with one hand, the boat with the other, and off they headed to do battle.

The old woman must have slinked away through the short grass when she saw this fiercesome duo approach because there wasn't another word said about it by anyone except me. Self-regulation is the best policy but it only works when properly applied. Stephen is allowed his boat with him down to the swimming pool early in the morning and later in the evenings, not in the afternoons when it is at its busiest.

Peter, throughout our journey but most especially since our arrival in Spain, has shown a remarkable ability with direction, road layout and generally finding our way to and from wherever. After four or five days driving around here I am only just beginning to grasp in my mind's eye what appears to have come naturally and almost immediately to him. Caroline, with the aid of her maps was a great help, in getting lost. This is unfair, we normally took a wrong turn which sent us on our way somewhere else and as Caroline always squealed:

"It's your fault, you're driving too fast!"

Yes, I always was driving too fast, it's compulsory out here. My own excuse for not being able to immediately grasp what was what in terms of road layout out here was I had driven too far for too long, too fast for my head to be of any use to myself or anyone else for that mater. If truth be told my brain had felt like scrambled egg for a lot longer than the holiday. Thomas, as is his wont, took the back seat literally as well as metaphorically; Rebecca was the same except metaphysically as well as as well. So, a ghost was driving, a shadow was directing and, as is normal in life, everything was in the hands of the gods, as was definitely the case with our reading of the signposts that weren't there.

We have by now settled nicely into this mode of doing nothing, in fact I could happily go on doing this nothing business for, oh, let me see now, another week perhaps. Well, what is there to do? That is my exact point – relax. What the heck does 'relax' mean? Relax for me is what I did on my way home from work knowing and feeling I was tired after completing a thoroughly satisfying nine, ten or eleven hour stint of good graft; knowing that everything was hunky dory and would remain so until my return early the following morning.

What a plonker I have been for too many years now for in reality I was too stressed out to relax, too tired to enjoy my family, to worn out to teach my family, too many sore heads to be with my family, too much work to be a real part of my own family. I would sometimes take them out, I would more often join them somewhere but rarely would I actually be with them, be an active part of them. After working from before seven in the morning I would take the occasional afternoon off from around one or two o'clock and we would head off in the wagen to the beach or to a relative's or friend's house and while they did whatever I would sit down or lie down and sleep. It is time to waken up. It is time to change all that before I'm too old and they're gone or vice versa.

At the moment I can't even go out onto the patio for lunch without staring at the tits on the big healthy woman laid out on her lounger next door, well, you have to stare don't you? It would be bad manners not to have a good goggle. The silly thing is that it is overcast today and therefore there is little to no chance of her getting even a faded freckle on one of her thingameboobs warmed not to mention tanned. Still, it's very good of her to offer up her pale whatever you call them for public countenance and scrutiny. I hope it is sinking into my boys that there has to be more to a woman than two taps and a plughole. How she sounds, smells, feels, along with any other attributes she may have will become important in time as add-ons to how she looks; the boys will have to know it is only by digging really deep that they will stand a chance of finding one of the true gems. First of all though, they have to learn to dig deep within themselves if they are to learn to understand how to find if their other sort has any depth, daring and do. Before that they might need glasses and other restructuring work to their eyes to compensate for the malalignment they suffer every time they walk out into the garden to move a piece of garden furniture to its newly corrected position; or one of those surgical collars to compensate for the strain on their necks as they 'eyes left' every time they head down to the pool. That's my boys!

We headed down the road this afternoon to Gibraltar and, according to Stephen today is Monday 5th August and he should know because he has a watch. I had heard that the Spanish road sign makers association was particularly unhappy with the fact that the Union Jack still held sway over this tiny but in some way significant outcrop of rock and in their huff they refused to write its name anywhere. It wasn't until we were virtually there, when we could actually see the place, that a road sign appeared directing us to it. Isn't that quaint? What was even quainter was the last half mile of our journey taking over one and a half hours. Low and behold on the way back out it took us one and a half hours to complete the first half mile. We had learned our lesson though and were well prepared for our journey back out just as we were unprepared for the enormous delay on the way in. For the return journey we stopped at a BP filling station to arm ourselves with cool water, cans and whatever the children wanted and I filled the wagen up with diesel. I cannot remember fuel ever being so cheap, sixty odd litres cost 22.39 sterling. Now, I ask you, would you want to join up with something you are already joined to and thus lose your tax free lustre overnight? Not a chance.

The long queues of traffic in and out of the rock are caused by mean spirited Spanish policemen who feel this is the best way to get back at – tourists? I know it is not the policemen's fault they are mean spirited, they cannot help being the way they are, it is the Spanish government who have obviously gathered all their mean spirited policemen together and exiled them to as far away a place they could manage, and this just happens to be border duty with Gibraltar. This was the only time in all our travels we were asked to produce our passports.

Gibraltar, it is a great big lump of rock alright and there's no doubting its strategic value in 1704, or in 1804, or even in 1904 but that is as far as it goes. We took a ride on the cable car up the side of the rock and that made Caroline tremble, it just made the rest of us nervous. What a disappointment it was when we got to the top. It was a quarter to five and the restaurant, shop and apes closed at four-thirty. There wasn't a single ape, monkey or whatever they aren't, to be seen at all, this was a great disappointment for the children. They were almost as disappointed by this as we all were by the restaurant being closed. The whole place seemed run down, neglected, which is bad because it does not take a lot of effort to keep a place clean and tidy and a coat of paint would certainly not have gone amiss either. I hope the air of neglect does not extend to maintenance on the mechanics of the cable car, now the thought of that is enough to make you tremble.

I feel that the rock of Gibraltar should not be given back to Spain, nor should the British be allowed to keep it. It should instead be given to the French, for at least three years, so much more efficient are they at running these national monuments than anyone else in Europe.

An interesting fact about Gibraltar was gleaned when I took a wrong turn – nothing new there I hear you say – and kept on going to see where it led to. This was over at the far side of the rock, past the lighthouse and the Arabesque looking church. There were a couple of big lorries turning into a cordoned off area and they were the only traffic on this narrow road; on up through the 'no entry' signs we went, turned the wagen at the entrance to an old military something or other, one of the roads of which went straight into the rock and on the slow journey back down I had a good look at what the lorries were doing. They were dumping rubbish. Nothing too extraordinary in this except what they were doing to the rubbish. There was an enormous rotating and angled pushing, crushing and squeezing machine that crammed the rubbish into one of the big caves. Imagine, in this age of technical brilliance some enormous eejit has been paid to organise a scheme whereby the community's rubbish is pushed into a cave. Their real backwardness has to be the fact they have not made this into one of the main tourist attractions of the Rock; I'm sure a whole posse of eco nuts would queue for hours to catch a glimpse of this.

It is not every day the children get to see another continent, I've only ever had visual contact with one continent myself, so today was not every day as we all stood up on the highest point we were allowed and waved our hellos over to Africa. It looked a bit hazy over beyond therefore it was difficult to make out if anyone was waving back. So Gibraltar has been seen, done and left a small taste of disappointment. Well, it serves us right for going there in the first place.

Whilst going to and coming from Gibraltar we passed over a lot of bridges which had signs saying Rio this and Rio that. This must be a Spanish expression for 'dry up' because there wasn't a drop of water in any one of these Rios. They reminded me of those plentiful scenes from old western movies where the cowboy stumbles along behind his horse holding onto its tail, both having walked for days in the soaring heat along a dry riverbed, his saddle, gun belt and water container having long since been dumped. In one of the many riverbeds we passed over they even had a couple of enormous mechanical diggers in doing a spot of maintenance work. I bet this sort of work dries up during winter.

Chapter Ten

Mixing

Three phone calls in one night, they are like buses, there isn't one for ages and then three come along together. Two of them were from mother, making sure we were still alive and the other was from friends Anne and Brian saying they and theirs were safely deposited in Torremolinos which is not too great a distance up the road and a day together has been arranged for the apartment today – I am writing this in the early hours of. I must say I am looking forward to the company, the craic and any news from home and it always does Caroline a power of good to have a friend to wine with.

Well, friends and theirs are here four or five hours now and Caroline and Anne are right and jolly which is hardly surprising given the amount of wine and sun consumed. They are away back for their second stint in the swimming pool after giving up begging, badgering and bothering me about joining them. It took Anne a while until she realised that swimming pool is not down on my list of things to do and certainly not at five o'clock in the day when the whole world and its mother are down there enjoying the sunny delights of thirty-seven degrees; definitely not my idea of cooling off.

"You have to learn to relax", is a favourite expression of Anne's and she does right to keep chirping it at me. Of course I need to learn to relax; I don't smoke, don't drink, don't play any sport these past number of years since my body gave in to the increasing demands of work, weight and age. I do what needs to be done and I do not complain. Out here I am away from most family and friends. I am away from a lot of the life that has long held interest for me. I make the best of it as I try to with all situations. From day start to day finish I do for my family in a way that probably surprises them. I take a lot of joy from the happiness that shows on Caroline's and the children's faces when we do what they want to do.

Back to our visitors then and poor Anne is laid up in bed after the after-effects of too much wine and too much sun. I think it was the one, she says it was the other, so we'll settle on both. I prepared and made the dinner and Caroline came out to lend a hand and with one stir of the pot my mushroom, peppers, onion, garlic and Ragu sauce mix splattered all over the tiles behind the cooker; definitely not too much sun with Caroline. At least Caroline did manage to eat a bit of dinner, needless to say Anne didn't make it up for any.

I have decided that the best way to compensate for my awaywardness is to change the wagen for a car when we get back, the idea being it will side-track my mind and give me something to chew on when the need takes out here. It is great, has worked a treat and has probably bored all others who come in contact with me out of their mind, apart from the boys. It is fantastic value for money too in terms of how it has drawn my attention away from the mundane and banal subexistence of holiday life. Fortunately Stephen, car fiend that he is, has brought along three car magazines including the August edition of Top Gear which is brilliantly informative and just fantastic to have in terms of something interesting to stick my head into away from the heat of the heat.

I tell you what though, you don't need much in the line of clothes around here, a statement that is even truer of the female species; a pair of sandals and a pair of shorts, a couple of shirts and a good hat is about all you need. My heavy cotton, wide brimmed, Australian bush type hat has proved indispensable since I bought it in Blois. Oh, how my heart yearns for Blois! Enough of that nonsense!

The world most certainly is ill-divided, so much rain for some, so much sun for others; so much pain for some, so much joy for others. Back home I know which category we fall into and I am more and more coming round to feeling I don't want to go back to that. It is not yet ten o'clock in the morning and we are sitting in the shaded patio area of the garden having our very simple breakfast of slices of fruits and a couple of different types of bread toasted plus our inimitable pot of tea made with our own blend of tea bag from home, Sainsbury's green tea or something. Caroline is hard at work with her 1987 copy of Berlitz travel guide to Costa del Sol and Andalusia – I bet there's been a few changes in its photographs over the past fifteen years – trying to locate somewhere of interest for us to go to today; my only insistence being that after our stagnation yesterday we get in a good walk wherever we go today.

Being good to yourself most of the time if not all of the time is fraught with anxieties too unless you are lucky enough to be stupid enough not to care. The main difficulty here comes in continuing the variety of pleasures you have to offer yourself not just on a daily basis but on a throughout the day basis as well. Perhaps the bodies who lie prostrate at the pool have it worked out, do one thing day in day out and in this way life is uncomplicated. Therefore you do not have to work out a schedule of where to go, what to take with you, what to do when you get there, plus all the multiplications of this scenario when you are functioning on the basis of eight.

Peter stands between two worlds. He has a pack of playing cards in

one hand and a toy plane he and Stephen each bought the other day in the other hand. He is looking for someone to play poker with but he has his toy as back up. Thomas wants to have staring competitions with whoever he eyes up. Stephen spends a lot of time amusing himself, often at the expense of others. Rebecca suffers withdrawal symptoms if she is away from a mirror for more than half an hour; this problem is only got round when she is in an area of population and has a lot of eyes staring back at her. The twins, Sarah and Emma, are two miniature grannies who busy themselves with whatever they can push their noses into. Caroline is greatly taken with the rays of hope emanating from the reddish colour beginning to relocate itself from the stratosphere and onto her legs.

I got my walk today, not a big distance in terms of what we walk at home but this must have amounted to five times that when the effects of sun and heat are worked into the equation. Bella Modena again but this time we were taking a good look at it. It was probably a resort in its own right at some stage in the past but it has been absorbed into the rest of the concrete package along the length of the coast. According to the electronic thermometer on the promenade the temperature was a mere 31°C while we were out walking. I think the breeze must have cooled the thermometer a bit because there was quite a strong wind blow factor and although its effect was quite enthusing it did little to lessen the strength of the sun. This was a hot hot day to walk the four or five miles we managed at the height of the day before taking refuge in a McDonald's for two cones, two large Coca Cola Light and six McFlurrys. Since Dime bars didn't make it this far south of the Pyrenees the children have had to mollify their lust with Smarties instead. Life sure feels a lot better after half an hour of air-conditioned respite washed down with cool drinks and topped off with ice cream.

To enlighten you as to how hot our walking exertions were, I carry the cool bag on all our excursions and from it today we sank two two litre bottles of Diet Pepsi and a one and a half litre of still water before ever McDonald's was mentioned as a pit stop. After ice cream and drinks there we had to stop at a shop for further replenishment before we got the length of the wagen. Another two one and a half litre bottles, one water, one lemon, were consumed before the car door opened.

As soon as we got back to the apartment Caroline and the children headed straight to the pool while I made dinner. I keep wondering when I am going to get fed up with all this pasta and vegetable eating, but there is no sign of this happening yet. I know if I was to do this back in the land of rain it wouldn't be long before I'd be looking for my normal bite and chew.

I've worked it out, the more stars there are in a film the greater chance there is of it being a crap show. One star means it's an excellent show; two stars mean it's a bit comme ci comme ca, it can go either way; more than two stars mean they are relying on the big names to hold the show together and when that happens, forget it. Chances are they have used up the bulk of the budget on the names instead of the special effects, good script, music and all the real bits that need to blend properly to make a good film great.

Caroline has just informed me that a Chinese takeaway with fried rice has over two thousand calories. I judge by the way she said it that this must be a lot so I tried to look suitably horrified. I could feel the fat in my belly cringe at the thought of having to share an already overcrowded area with more of its own type of molecules. Which brings me to one of my last thoughts of the early morn before I wrestle myself off this lazy chair and down to bed. Why does no one order a Chinese takeaway for breakfast? Don't say it's because they're not open, you know what I mean. There must be enormous sales potential here. Perhaps they should get the guy from McDonald's who came up with their early call menu to do them out something special; a vindaloo surprise would get them going early in the morning. It's amazing some of the early conversations that go on between wife and husband. I'm off to bed.

Today is a new day and guess what, it is sunny sun sun as per usual. I am still trying to work out whether it is the lack of doing anything productive that I abhor more than just the exercise in sun adoration itself. Sitting about in the heat is great so long as I am shaded from the direct sharpness of the sun. Caroline and Rebecca have taken to spending as much daylight as possible lying on their sun loungers facing the direct sunlight in a state of vegetative amnesia and this is absolute anathema to me. We are off soon up a mountain to see if we can find a bit of Spain.

Mijas – at last we have arrived in Spain. It is a quaint little white washed town not more than ten miles away. What has saved it from a life in death of holidaymakers is that most of the ten mile distance is straight up a mountain. Unfortunately for Caroline we approached it from the wrong side, the scenic side, the spiralling countryside road that was a bit too narrow and a bit too sheer on one side of the road for her liking. The town itself is a tourist shopper's paradise with everything from the Gucci Gucci range to the crappi crappi stuff. Caroline decided she needed a new purse in one of the half decent shops and then when we walked on and found one of the really good shops she realised she needed a new handbag. We must have been in and out of fifty different shops with their assorted wares all on show on the pavement. The children managed to acquire a motley assortment of presents for others, prizes for themselves, plus those indispensables that catch children's eyes, hold their imagination and concentrate their brainwaves on the positively, definitely must have.

On the way up in the wagen something caught my ear. First of all I thought there was something wrong with the engine or exhaust. Next I thought there must be a traditional strimming competition taking place with brilliantly camouflaged contestants, the whole way up the mountainside. Then I thought no, it's an invasion of the hissing whistlers or maybe even worse, an invasion of the wissing histlers. Finally Caroline enlightened me that the noise was being made by crickets. The poor little things must have been absolutely bursting with the horn and thus the extravagant calling out for a mate or else these were shrieks of pain as they face meltdown in the blaze of the afternoon sun.

Up at the head of the town we rested for a short time in the children's play park so they could practice their acrobatic skills and we could find some respite from the glare of the sun under the shade of the trees. It's not often you find trees with built in sound effect especially when there is not a whistle of wind but the crickets must have sought refuge thereabouts as well as they were blazing away overhead. Over on one side of the park there was the most spectacular view over the whole coastal arena from Bela Modena to Fuengirola and it was only but right and fitting that Mijas should be looking down on these other resorts. Between the two, going down the steps of the mountainside there was a glorious array of haciendas on the very grandly built size, each with a sparkling bright blue swimming pool attached.

The long and windy road that leads from the coast all the way up the mountain had displayed every so often what looked like circus type posters with dates and names on them as well as pictures of what could well be very butch looking flamenco dancers wearing funny black hats. On closer inspection these posters seemed to show the Spanish have a pretty ambivalent attitude toward young men and their wearing fancy sequenced costumes. Totally unrelated to this since it was built in 1900, a time before transskirties and transhighheelites, is the high whitewashed wall of the bullring in the centre of Mijas. A bullring, I must explain, is an arena where young men who suffer from only being able to walk by shuffling their feet along – it is obviously caught from penguins although, I must admit, you don't see a lot of these in Spain – are as a punishment made to wear Napoleon Bonaparte lookalike hats and try to redeem something from the family's male gene by sticking skinny swords into a drugged bull who has obviously snorted so much his mind is out of it. It may not look like a fair fight and I doubt indeed if it ever is, one being anything from five to ten times the weight of the other but something tells me the torreadors are safe enough from getting a tear or even a ladder in their tights.

I am beginning to fall into the way of these days which is pretty close to coming to enjoy them. My favourite part is still coming back from our run away, getting the dinner cooked and devoured and sitting down with my pen while the rest of the family flee to the swimming pool, before we all settle down to an evening of entertainment with a hired dvd. Last night's piece of Hollywood magic starred Robert Redford and Brad Pitt but don't ask me what it was called, 'Spy Game' or something I think. Tonight's offering stars Bruce Willis and is called 'Bandits' and it should be a decent action yarn. I love the togetherness of the family as the three older ones jostle for position on the couch and the three younger ones fight each other for closest proximity to their mother. It definitely must be love, certainly on Caroline's part, because she always ends up scranning extra sweets, chocolate, popcorn or whatever is on the go from whichever of the younger ones is on her lap at that time. Normally Sarah and Emma cannot make it though the two hour sitting and have to be carried off to bed, which means Stephen has his mother all to himself.

Even in the short space of time we have been out here there is the feeling that the nights are getting ever so slightly longer. What is left of daylight leaves it almost impossible to continue writing without the aid of an electric light and it is only – I had to go down to the bedroom to see what the time is - nine o'clock in the evening. Then again, as I look outside it seems bright enough, light into the apartment isn't great when the floodlight effect of the sunshine has been turned off.

The days are also drawing to a close on our time spent here with only four or five days left in Spain but as time rolls on I find myself becoming more and more at peace with the place. Perhaps I'm becoming more and more at peace with myself and that lets me tune in to life here better. Then, just as I feel myself relaxing into the swing of things I think I ought to go up to the apartment above and snatch the shoes off the person – a woman, I hope – who has been practising some form of military drill up and down, up and down on the marble floor wearing her stiletto heels.

In terms of annoyance this is second only to the poor seven month old baby next door whose consistency of crying could soon be entered in the Guinness Book of Crying because it cries morning, noon and night, as well as in the wee small hours of the morning. I feel I should jump over the fence and shove one of the child's mother's ample bosoms into its mouth, she being the one who always has them out on parade for the sun and whatever else to shine upon. Perhaps they have been out in the sun a bit too long and have developed a tough crispiness that the baby finds difficult to appreciate. The hermit that's in me reacts a bit to this communal living lark. I've got the sounds of the crickets in my head, they are like wind up toys in terms of the sound the winding mechanism makes when it is unwinding. They will all go.

Mother was on the phone tonight. It is great to hear her yet hearing her voice makes me yearn for home. This has been cured somewhat by mother telling me they have had two days good weather in the past week, which can probably be extended to the past month. The rain, I freely admit, I do not miss; the sun, I freely admit, is a blessing.

Understanding is coming to me of why so many holiday so often. When you think of it it is a very good idea to get up whenever you feel like it after going to bed at whatever time took your fancy, add to this the fact that you do whatever you like during the day, going wherever you want to. I am beginning to feel the benefits of this in myself and hopefully this has been apparent to the family over the past number of days too. This is me coming from my angle where I kinda like who I was and although I knew I was working too hard I still didn't mind doing what I was doing. Just imagine then what it's like for those who don't like who they are and do mind what they do whether they work or not, coming out here where everyone is stripped down to the bare minimum, must come as a source of great relief to them.

Add to this escapism the fact that if you're an old stick in the mud like me it's nice sitting, walking and working in a very pleasant heat, day in day out. It is more than nice having sunshine pour into your life from every part of the heavens for at least ten hours a day. The eternal drizzle at home is not conducive to happiness, is not conducive to good lifestyle, is not conducive to harmony in society. How many times have I said "if the weather's good this afternoon we'll head off – wherever", knowing that in all probability I would be working all day because the rain, as usual, was on for the duration. We are a society of fools for living in such awful climate conditions in the first place. When away from it all it is a lot easier to have misgivings about the situation we come from. Isn't it much more sensible finding ways of cooling ourselves down instead of trying always to keep ourselves warm? It is no great wonder why so many attempt to brighten up their lives by means of drugs, alcohol or whatever it takes to put a bit of brightness into their lives. A lot of the social problems at home are definite side-effects of trying to make escape from the low brow life that passes for living, for a lot of nonsense that make up people's lives.

Someone has informed me that today is Friday 9th August which is of absolutely no significance out here (apart from the fact that this day next week will be Caroline's birthday) the days being all the same with one as glorious as the next. All six children are avid poker players now courtesy of my teaching them. We play for matches now but later in life I'll teach them how to play for money; the importance of this comes in the form of not only teaching you a lot about yourself but also providing a genuine insight into the true nature of others, little things that otherwise years of living or working with might never unveil. At the moment it's great for the children, beefing out their characters.

Caroline is so taken with the idea of having nice brown legs I think it is the reason behind her wanting to stay here an extra day next week and driving straight up through Spain by way of Madrid to our first stop in Bergerac in the southern realms of France. This is a hefty drive. Doing it with plenty of sleep the night before and without the hassle of a break-in on the morning of should avoid any headaches after we arrive. It is not a good idea but I will go along with it; anything to help brown those legs.

As arranged we had the day in Torremolinos with friends Anne and Brian and theirs but it was all a bit on the cramped side until we headed out into the town in the evening. First of all we went and visited their daughter Hannah and her cousin Emily in the bar where their summer work keeps them vampired (they work from around eight o'clock in the evening to five or six o'clock in the morning). We then walked around the town, Caroline and Rebecca already having managed to purchase a couple of pairs of sandals each – their suitcases must by now have got over the shock of the Toulouse theft – and I had my second purchase of the holidays, a new pair of sunglasses. My old sunglasses are great, I've had them for years, keep them in their case and look after them properly and they'll still be great for wearing at home when you put them on for a short spell whilst driving or sitting out or in somewhere sunny. They are full metal framed and wearing them each and every day with the continuous sunshine has left the skin on the bridge of my nose feeling as if it is about to split every evening. Now I can adorn my eyes with plastic frameless sunglasses, which I could wear for a month at a time.

The evening walk around Torremolinos was the highlight of the day with shops open to all hours of the night, with pedestrians cramming the narrow streets with their casual evening walkabout. Every short distance there were professional, semi-professional and very unprofessional bands, groups and individuals doing their thing every thereabouts. Every bar with its plastic seats and tables out front advertising different European brews was worked by eighteen to twenty-four year old slim girls of white, west European extraction. As we moved on down the side streets, stalls took over from shop fronts and the range of goods on sale became more upmarket while the guys selling at the stalls became a lot darker in colour. The upmarket goods they were selling were sunglasses made by Gucci, Cartier and such like for the amazingly affordable price of nine Euro each. Other stalls along our way were marketing Rolex and other delightfully dear makes of watch for ten Euro each. I cannot understand why they weren't queued out with customers, then again perhaps only so many bargains can be sold in a given place at a given time. Some chance!

It was around midnight when we left Torremolinos, the streets were still packed with every sort out wandering and walking about and it was very obvious that a lot of these were families, some with young children, some with very young children. The restaurants and bars were still quite full with people enjoying their dinner, just about six hours too late, followed by drink after drink, taking in all the goings on in the relaxed feel of a balmy August night. Balmy is one way to describe the night air for at this hour of the morning it is still 32°C. I cannot say it felt much hotter during the day but temperatures like this in the early hours of the morning only happen once or twice a year back home and only when Caroline and myself have gone out for the evening to return home in the early hours of the following morning to find the children have gone to bed leaving the central heating on. The children loved the night-time walk around the streets and characters and goings on and different way of living and general buzz that was evident in every one of the narrow streets and wide squares. It really opened their eyes as to how the other half live: "This is better than a dvd" is how they described it to me.

If there is such a thing as reincarnation I have decided that I'm coming back in my next life as a sun lounger, not the person but the plastic object. Women are very taken with them, in fact they become very attached to them, lie on top of them for great lengths of time at a time, this way up, that way down, over on one side, then the other, arms all over them, legs all round them, body pressed into them, dreams dreamt on them; an inordinate amount of pleasure for such an inanimate object, and this is meant both ways round.

I still cannot understand how a woman can reach the relatively tender age of two score and two, in one week's time, without before having noticed she had a pair of legs. You can understand someone not noticing if they only had one leg, but two, there's absolutely no excuse for not noticing two of them. Since last week a fortune of oil, time, sun and staring has gone into the great bronzing of Caroline's legs and it is beginning to pay off; I don't believe the topic of conversation will change for a very long time to come.

Back to Puerto Banus this afternoon 39°C. Wow! Hot it most certainly is. The trick is to keep drinking, keep pouring the cool stuff down you and then hop into as many air conditioned establishments as possible which, of course, happen to be commercial premises. The more Caroline and the children see of this place the more they love it; the more they see of other resorts, the more they love here even more than they already loved it. It is that bit more up market that leaves it a lot less densely populated than the overcrowded resorts. The girls all love it here because of the shops with everything from the expensive to the outrageously expensive. The boys love it because it is a living, modern car museum, no matter which direction you look you see mechanical luxury in all its beautiful glory. I love it because it has something for everyone and therefore pleases all who have constant smiles shining out. It is nice too that we can go somewhere handy where all our expectations are surpassed.

The boys and twins are down making waves in the swimming pool, they'll be back soon for dinner, which is being prepared tonight by a comedy double act, called Caroline and Rebecca. Much as in the mould of Morecambe and Wise there is a lot of silly banter going on, a few squeals, pushes and shoves, a fair bit of "Oh no you won't" and "Oh yes I will"; plus the dropping and pushing around of props, both vegetable and metal, in the kitchen. Some of the props they wear; Caroline is barefoot in bathing suit; Rebecca is high-heeled, short skirted, skimpy-topped, with bandana wrap on head. Caroline has the lead part and Rebecca is her straight side-kick who is used to do this, taste that, hold these, go outside with those; the replies are generally in the negative which explodes the routine down a new comedic line.

The smell of curry is wafting all over me from the kitchen and making me even hungrier than I thought I was. An absolute delicious treat of chicken, curried sauce mixed with red and green peppers, onions, mushrooms, garlic, basmati rice, oven chips and green beans or whatever you call those elongated green, watery bits that resemble elasticated pea-pods. Top this off with a Coca Cola Light drink they sell out here with a green cap, I think this my preferred drink of the season has a twist of lime in it which makes a nice lively difference to taste and I am a happy man.

The difference between life and living out here and life and living at home is that as much as possible is performed in the great bright outdoors here while as much as possible has to be performed in the dark and dreary indoors at home. We spend a lot of time, effort and money on our homes in an effort to brighten up our daily existence. Out here people spend a lot of time, effort and money on themselves because mother nature has been so good to have brightened up their daily existence in the first place. Sunshine really must be the elixir of life. It brightens, satisfies, nourishes, strengthens, replenishes, in fact it does everything good and positive needed for a healthy existence.

Rain dulls, depresses and just about washes all the goodness, well being and sense of good living out of our existence with its incessant battering of the senses. So persistent has it been in our weather patterns of recent times it has left us with little else to think of because there is little else to remember in weather terms. It isn't so long ago I can remember we used to have Spring that was showery but warming.

Summer that was warm but showery; Autumn when it rained and got colder; Winter when cold turned our rain to ice and snow and thence back to rain again. Now we are consumed by one long indeterminate season where the temperature moves from low cool to high cool, when the rainfall changes from bearable incessant to incessant unbearable. This is the truth of it now, rainfall which is the central strain of our weather patterns does not change, it stays more or less exactly the same. Unfortunately, it will probably take a couple of generations for the fine tuning button inside the head of we the people of the rainy north to adapt until we finally accept our new predicament. This is unfortunate for north-west European man because it comes at a time in human existence terms when we are being made spoil ourselves more and more. So, more and more planes and boats will be heading off more and more often to sunny climes; this is the only answer for now.

The returnees are on their way back in from the evening swimming session. They are extra keen on their soft seat tonight because our big screen offering is a dvd of 'Rat Race' staring Rowan Atkinson and such like cast in a madcap comedy which is exactly to the children's liking. I also managed to acquire six packets of Fruit Pastilles this morning in a little out of the way shop, which has made them enormously happy, a little treat from home.

It is another day, I know that much; it could be Sunday; it may be Sunday; it probably is Sunday; it must be Sunday. Must be comes from the viewpoint of those who claim to be in the know about these matters. I'll find out for definite later when I buy a Sunday newspaper, I hope. We are entertaining this afternoon and evening as Anne, Brian and two boys Peter and Daniel are coming over; dinner is already made for the adults so it'll just be a throw together oven pizzas and chips for the children.

The bathroom got a bit crowded there; Rebecca, like any normal person, likes her privacy and prefers to use it on her own, so it was with howls of distain that she greeted an intrusion upon her privacy. It was something with more legs than a horse, two antennae like old fashioned television top aerials, a harder shell to crunch than a lobster and coloured a darker shade of black than the rain soaked contents of your average coal bunker back home. I tried to be nice to it and lift it out on a table mat but the little blighter must have a lot of Skippy blood in its legs because it jumped about fifty times its body height, higher than I did. In the end it got the message and went quietly enough, suffering the ignominy and whatever else of a free fall parachute jump over the far side of the garden wall; well, I presume it had a parachute.

It is Sunday. I was up at the Supersol supermarket and I saw a few newspapers, too few in fact, so it must be Sunday. The place is so busy on a normal day but on a Sunday most of the little shops around the place don't open and the other Supersol supermarket fifteen yards away from this one doesn't open either. Mayhem is what follows. People hereabouts, holidaytakers and other such blends of escapees, have to shop on a daily go get it fresh basis which gives some of them something useful to do and others a raison d'etre. So here they all are, squashed in together, only problem is I am obviously here with the late risers so all that is good is gone. I don't think there's much point in me buying a German newspaper.

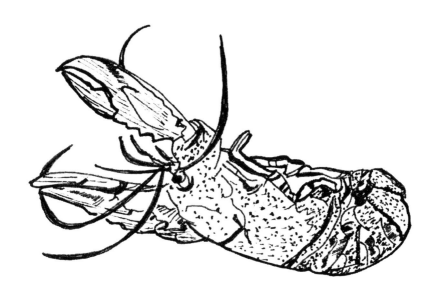

Sunshine. It provides dizzy relief and hot hope for the blond masses. They absolutely adore its power to change them from the fat, feckless, ugly, white blobs they spend so much of their life complaining to and about into the fat, feckless, ugly, bronzed blobs they become. For eleven months of the year it gives them hope and expectation; for two weeks of the year it gives them a clear shot at themselves, at making right all the wrongs of their recent life.

How on earth can so little please so many for so short a space of time? So much so they cannot wait to come back for more, well that's hardly surprising. I know I've a nerve to talk about these the enormous questions of life and I can say now with real certainty it is a good thing I didn't go away on holiday for so long because I doubt whether I could have returned home to being the workaholic prat I was. There must be something good about holidays since so many people go on them, just as there must be something good about smoking since so many people smoke, just as there must be something good about golf, about drinking, about gambling, about obesity. Human nature is frail and is fraught with all the disadvantages of self that can be thought of, plus those that haven't yet been thought of. We are masters of our own oblivion and yet we are oblivious to it, in that much we are lucky. Regarding paleness of skin as some form of imperfection is something I am oblivious to, skin is skin whatever way it comes, it has its nice points just as it has its not so perfect features as well. I'll take it whatever way it is, if others want it to glow a bit then that'll do fine and dandy as well.

Which brings me back to the reality of my own situation in that our beautiful accommodation is in a nice, quiet, family orientated part of the coast. That is the upside; the downside is that families mean children and children mean babies and babies mean noise, a lot of noise, an awful lot of noise when you are long used to the peace and quiet of no crying at home. Babies, as with children, should be more like televisions with a mute button, which can be worked by any television remote control. The genetic modifiers could in time add a mood button for teenagers. Now that would be interesting. For now we'll have to continue keeping them well nourished and entertained to maximise their smiles.

Here the dvd comes in handy for the younger lot during siesta time. At the height of the heat of the day all the extra scenes, background detail, interviews and director's cut make wonderful entertainment for the children sometimes because they are genuinely interested in the film but mainly because they can understand it, it is in English. Occasionally, in the late morning or early evening, they'll sit and flick through the television stations of which there are around fifteen, hoping to catch a glimpse of a familiar face in The Simpsons, Buffy the Vampire Slayer or Scooby Doo that have been the three and only success stories to date. After about ten minutes the Spanish is so disconcerting to the senses it gives them new impetus to go out and enjoy the swimming pool again.

I have to keep telling myself, it is another cracker day weather wise today, I think I could never be out here long enough for the novelty of constant good weather to wear off. I have decided after buying a couple of Sunday newspapers to provide some conversation relief that they provide more annoyance than amusement, more infuriation than information, in fact they are but a complete waste of time. This is fine if you have plenty of time to waste, indeed in this way they become indispensable to some. I am reverting back to my old way of being which is that they do not deserve my time or interest in them, my observations or even my oversight.

People go and people come in the apartments around and above and new faces mean new sounds. It is strange how in the day before they leave the departees suddenly come over all friendly and in five minutes over the fence or wall or in the car park you get their whole life story interspersed with all the disasters of this or that holiday plus anything else that has gone wrong in their past half lifetime. I suppose I could have been a bit friendlier toward them, just as I suppose I could be a bit more accommodating toward the sun and lie out under its rays and let it shade my epidermis but if I don't feel like doing it why the hell should I? I am sure they are all very nice, interesting, wonderful people but on a need to know basis, they don't need to know me.

Chapter Eleven

Last Orders

It is Monday and yes you have guessed it, the sun is shining and the children are in a hurry to get to the pool; Rebecca is torn between two worlds, two needs, she wants to go to the pool and enjoy the fun and splashing about with her siblings and others but she wants to work on her sun tan as well. As every woman knows a suntan can only successfully be accomplished with bottles of before, during and after lotion, lots of applications of each plus the indispensable lie on your back and belly for hours at a time staring up at the wide blue yonder or down through the plastic of your lounger. Caroline has now joined our eldest in this woman's quest for outer goldliness. In preparation for this momentous event in life women have a practice run at Christmas by

cooking as big a turkey as their oven will allow. In the performance of this ritual it is necessary to baste the beast to encourage an all round cooked effect with proper browning and crisping of the skin. Isn't it wonderful how imitation can imitate the imitators.

It would seem that a bunch of DIY enthusiasts of whatever extraction have moved into the apartment above. While we were sitting out on the patio last night they started work on theirs, with great gusto I might add but at least they were happy, laughing and cavorting as they did it. This morning not only have they been cleaning, you know that brushing noise as they try to get right into the corners that your ears pick up so well as you lie in bed under the sound; and now they have started to drill. I might be wrong here, perhaps a dentist's surgery has opened above us; this could be fortuitous as one of my big molars at the top has been giving me trouble again and Eric, my intrepid man with the drill is unfortunately a couple of thousand miles away. Ah, the drilling has stopped, he must be filling in the holes now.

Caroline has induced our youngest son Stephen into rubbing one of her wonder solutions into the awkward areas of her back. Stephen finds his new role in life particularly amusing just as he finds amusement and fun in almost everything he does and most definitely in everything that those around him do, with specific reference here to his teachers. Lucky guy, I hope it lasts.

We hit four wheel drive country today. No,

not the city school run for the worried mothers with their precious cargo of one point four little whatevers. Ronda. It's a beautiful town down the coast and up up up up up the mountain. We are talking mountain here and we are talking windy road. No, not your quaint little bendy bits that some of our countryside roads have at home for two or three miles. We are talking rising at least a couple of thousand feet on a bendy road that goes on and on, not for five miles, not for ten miles, not for fifteen miles, not even for twenty miles, but for over twenty-six miles. I bet they don't have anything like this in Disneyland Paris, Florida or where ever else they are planning to deculturalise. I bet they don't have anything like this on the Monte Carlo Grand Prix circuit or any other Grand Prix circuit you could name.

Apparently this road was only built about twenty years ago and it has knocked about one hour of travel time off for the locals when they're running down to their nearest seaside resort for an ice-cream. On one side of the road is steep rocky mountainside concreted in some places, wire mesh over it in other places and signs warning of rock falls in between. On the other side of the road there is nothing, that's right, it just falls away off the face of the earth. This provided great fun for the kids and myself on the way back down as we played on Caroline's enormous fear of deep ravines or rather the hair-raising experience of driving around them.

As you may already have guessed the town of Ronda was originally built on the edge of a ravine and it thus provides us with a startling bridge built over this. One of the best and most easily defended positions in times of old warfare, the Spaniards around here must have learnt a few tricks over the centuries about making good in such arid conditions. It must take a great bit of organisation to sustain a large community at such a great height nowadays, so what must it have been like two or three centuries ago.

The town itself is a magical warren of narrow streets running off from the main square where the bullring and other buildings of note are gathered. There is very little in this the old part of town or in any of the newer parts of town that are not white washed and everywhere the buildings are either two or three stories tall. You can see the old Spain here, you cannot miss it, it is everywhere, it is all pervasive and yet you cannot taste it, but you can taste McDonald's which is right beside the bull ring. All the quaint little shops are air conditioned and fitted out with the same touristaphelia; tacky, supposedly locally fashioned and made pieces of ephemera (junk) which not even a bus load of blind Yanks would believe to be of local ethnic origin. I think the world has become wise to the machinations of tourist money hunters.

A busload of Japanese passed us out walking with their hats on and sunbrellas up, the temperature was in the early forties as the sun split the dry ground and yet not one of our little oriental flavoured friends donned a pair of sunglasses as they smiled their way past us but there was not one plastic, paper or any other type of shopping bag between the lot of them. There was not one ugly momento whether plastic, porcelain, metal or clay, all they had was cameras and camcorders at the ready, plus one big curly piece of sausage meat. Two Japanese men were nearly off their trolley with laughter after having an obviously delightfully funny piece of conversation probably regarding the origins, merits and possible uses of this enormous piece of meat. Maybe they were wondering what size of a cow's ass it had come out of. I hope they realised it had to be sliced first before any attempt was made to put it in the mouth.

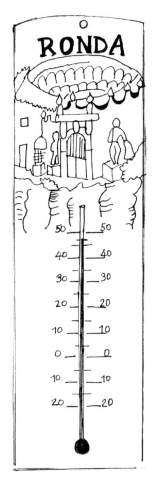

As I said before, cameras and camcorders were at the ready to take with them any little momentos in terms of moments or scenes that they wished to; the day of the tourist being taken in by cheap fakes and general trash is long gone for most. Judging by the amount still on sale it is not gone for all; judging by the reaction of our children, this age group is still a good target. Walking around Ronda in forty odd degrees of sunshine and heat drains the juice out of you very quickly, the high altitude not helping too much either, so a lot of cooling refreshment in the form of water, Coke Light and other liquids backed up by McFlurrys and ice pops were needed to keep us going.

After the family set down and dvd showing Caroline and I sat down at our map of Spain and we agreed to do a one shot back up Spain to Bergerac in the south of France. It will mean leaving early enough on Thursday morning but I am hoping the drive will be but a twelve-hour jaunt. If we find a McDonalds along the way things won't be so bad – I am only joking. No, I'm not. By now I have come to realise that a McDonald's sign on the horizon gives a wonderful sense of hope and a great feeling of relief in the nether region. The bold statement it makes is that there is a standard of toilet hygiene that is perfect for our needs and these facilities are there for our convenience even if we only buy a small bottle of water; in many cases we used their facilities without buying anything. It means there is a good basic range of food available, which is good value for money in France and excellent value for money in Spain.

You know that what you order is what you are going to get and in a time scale you couldn't match at home with all your preparation done beforehand. You know you will get a place to park, a place to sit; you can keep an eye on the children playing as well because they will always be finished before you they like it so much. If need be you can watch your car while eating, you can phone home also and not get ripped off by charges. Every McDonald's is an oasis of decent western standards you can rely on to support you from early morning until late in the evening seven days a week. Something I know from my work background is not easy to achieve and takes a lot of working at to maintain. God bless McDonalds!

Remember the tooth I mentioned yesterday? Well, it has bitten back. It is 5.25am and after lying in bed for over half an hour trying to toss and turn myself back to sleep I gave up, got up and now I am up, sitting in the lounge and the pain is quite real. Add to this the fact that some jerk-off is playing music not too far away in the apartment block and you'll know how I'm feeling. Only another four hours to hang about and wait until I can go out and try to find a dentist with a reasonable amount of English. Pain, I would hazard a guess, is universal and I hope the means of finding out about it and dealing with it are universal too.

There now, I have wasted another ten minutes going to the toilet and mixing up a mouthwash solution. When walking in one of the maze of side streets in Ronda yesterday and with the root of this tooth starting to wind me up, at two minutes to five in the early evening, or is it the late afternoon, a shutter was thrown up by an old lady as I passed. A big green fluorescent cross in a squared shape flickered to life and as I continued walking a glance above the door established this was a Farmacia. It took a few moments for me to consider but as my thoughts stumbled on up the narrow street I took this sign as a sign, well I would, wouldn't I? I took it as a sign that she was bound to have a mouthwash that was stronger and therefore ten times better than the normal green liquid we use at home and which I had been using thus far on holidays. I also took this as a sign that Caroline could go and ask for it since neither she nor I have a word of Spanish between us. I skipped over to the shop window that had attracted her attention and reflection and told her of my discovery. "Right", she said "come on girls" and off the four females headed acting as if it was the easiest thing in the world to go into a shop and buy something. Females really are amazing creatures.

While myself and the boys were standing twiddling our eyes over products and prices in the windows of shops that were still closed, I thought Caroline was giving the girls a lesson in the development of the species or is it the battle of the sexes? So I stood with the three boys and had a good bit of male bonding with them with comments along the line of: "What takes women so long to perform a perfunctory task such as this?" The boys were in total agreement with whatever I said. After fifteen minutes and still no sign of them coming out I thought the Farmacia must also be a Perfumerie as is the case quite often back home but not that I had noticed up until then in Spain. The boys and my lethargic self began a slow trot back down toward the little old lady's disappearing shutters. Low and behold as soon as we got there out pops the four of them looking bewildered but at least Caroline clutched a paper bag.

"Jeez, don't ever do that to me again", she blurted in a voice that mixed relief with exasperation. "That woman hadn't a word of English!"

My eyes indicated this was terrible, it shouldn't happen, I was sorry, she was wonderful, I was very brave considering the pain I could soon be suffering and I was and always would be eternally grateful to her for getting me something that would not only deprive me of the pain I would doubtless otherwise soon be in but this was bound to mean the rest of our holiday was going to be sweet and beautiful and wonderful and laced with honey.

Did I leave anything out?

The paper bag with the reassuring green pharmaceutical sign on the outside wasn't handed over immediately. I looked at Caroline. "It has to be mixed with water," and her eyes said it with the control of someone who obviously knew about these things. "Ah, it must be good then." I said, subjugated again. All hope for a speedy recovery from the infection I knew had already taken hold but which I still hoped against hope hadn't was contained in this simple paper bag. "It's the best." Caroline's air baked me with its defiant authority. Hope not only lives eternal but actually comes in floods at times of need such as this. So the sickly feeling of the inevitable approach of pain left and was replaced by the thought that I could have another ice-cream and deaden any interference this caused by using this wonderdrug mouthwash

immediately afterwards. Life didn't seem so terribly bad after all.

I'm sitting here thinking it has just gone half six in the morning and I don't think it would be so unreasonable of me to put the kettle on for a cup of tea and I could also have a slice of that tempting marble cake which looked so delicious and inviting that I thought I must rescue it from its lonely shelf life. If I put the kettle on to boil this might awaken someone in the apartment, most probably Caroline and this would be wrong even though it would enlighten her to my pain. For some reason the pain never seems as bad sitting up as it is when your head rests on your pillow probably because the mind can jump from one thing to another instead of concentrating wholly on its own misery. What to do now though, I don't think tea is the answer, it might enliven the infection. A pain as we all know is only half a pain unless we can share it with somebody but it's still too early for anyone else to be up; pity. I know, I'll pull over the pouffee for my feet and see if I can snooze a bit.

I heard a noise, I must have dozed off first of all and then I heard a noise. It sounded as though someone was carrying water and trying to get the key into their door lock next door. 'I'm sleeping,' I thought 'this is some weird dream'. But it continued. I opened my eyes slightly. The light was still on although the room was in brightness from the new dawn outside. I just wanted to close my eyes and go to sleep but what was my tooth doing? Now it really was beginning to manifest its dissatisfaction with the world. Now the throbbing was real and almost fully grown. I must get to a dentist.

What was that noise? Was it coming from outside or was someone at the metal shutters at the kitchen window with a bottle of water? What was going on because the kitchen windows are doubled glazed and closed so you wouldn't hear a sound like that or any other through them unless, unless they weren't closed, unless someone had managed to open them by some magical method of water movement and a bottle. Shit! I'd better get up and see.

I looked at the small digital reading at the side of the phone screen, 8.22; I must have slept for an hour, maybe an hour and a half but did I leave the kitchen door open or almost closed like it was now. I looked around, the door out of the dining area was wrong; I had left it fully open, now it was only open by about a foot. What was going on? The children were all quiet. If there's one of them up then they are all up. I moved slowly as I rose to get up. Shit! The cushion that was on my lap fell on the floor, it didn't make much of a noise but it was enough for me to notice and someone else might have heard its soft landing. I moved a few steps. Maybe I should go back down to the bedroom and put on a pair of trousers. I was standing naked but for my white Ys. Another couple of steps and I was at the kitchen. The noise grew louder and stranger still, it was like a deep throaty hissing noise. "Morning babe", I said sleepily, now for the first time I could taste the badness of the tooth awake in my mouth.

"I didn't want to waken you, you were asleep." It was Caroline. She was ironing.

It's amazing what goes through your head when you're not fully with it, which could be the case for a lot of people even at their best of times. "I have an antibiotic in the medicine tub", Caroline remarked nonchalantly. My eyes queried the word 'antibiotic'. "It was for Sarah. The one the dentist prescribed before she had that tooth pulled." My face obviously still hadn't made it out of sleep control mode. "I got the chemist not to make it up. It just needs water added. It's for a child so you take a double dose." Caroline saw that I still wasn't convinced. "It'll not kill you." She added emphatically.

I liked that last bit best, very reassuring, not. Caroline went and got the magic bottle from the plastic medicine tub which is crammed full of everything you wouldn't expect to see, not to mention use; contents befitting the chemists' daughter. Soon the magic bottle had become a magic potion and Caroline stood over me with a capful of bright yellow liquid. I smelt it. It smelt reassuringly for a child. I emptied the contents into my mouth and downed it in one. Get to work now you little yellow devils.

The four youngest are up now, the world of night-time has ended, the real world has begun again and so I have to divest myself of drowsy feelings of tiredness and pain and go and do what needs to be done. The children's minds are very firmly fixed on home this morning, their talk is on what they are going to do when they get back. Maybe the day has yet to warm them up to its charms. A visit to the swimming pool will very quickly extinguish any thought there is of home.

Tom phoned last night. Among his news was that he and his family are to be filmed over the next three to four months going about their daily activities. Filming will be roughly two days per week. The remit is they were looking for a professional family and they want to provide an insight into how they live. They are to be followed performing the perfunctory duties of living, working, playing and being whatever it is that they are. Tom is confident there will be no abuse of the privilege of letting them into their home life. I am not so sure. Personally I wouldn't trust them.

They are filming eight families from different social backgrounds but my feeling is that these guys see themselves as in the entertainment business albeit of a certain strain and they will feel they have to provide some meat for their viewers to eat. Is it likely then they are going to show how working class boy can do well through hard work, endeavour and passing a lot of exams? I think it much more likely they will concentrate on lifestyle – on big house, fancy cars, children's hobbies et al and how this will look when compared to ordinary lives; so what will it look like when compared to how a poor family lives? I wouldn't have them anywhere near me.

It is well after one o'clock and we are only back in from Puerto Banus where we had to go to get two electrical adaptors Tom asked me to get for him last night. Thanks Tom. The adaptors didn't even cost a couple of pounds but when you take wife and entourage into a hypermarket it costs you over seventy-five pounds. For some reason women feel it incumbent upon them to fill the trolley every time they go into a supermarket; it is like a feeling of destiny unfulfilled if they haven't something precariously positioned and about to fall off the top of the trolley.

Right now I am sitting looking at a lovely lunch having already taken my third double dose of children's antibiotic and I am thinking to myself this stuff must be slow to work for there ain't nothing happening yet.

I got to a dentist this afternoon and his English was excellent, his hearing was a bit suspect at times but what the heck, he was a dentist; he was German of course as was his mentality. I explained to him what the problem was and how Eric, my dentist, had spent the past couple of years trying to save this tooth, having spoken first of where I was from, about the holiday and where we were staying in the area.

"Ah, you English dentist are all the same." It could have come from anywhere because he was wearing a face mask. There was no point in trying to challenge any of his assertions as one of his rubber hands rested in my open gob. "Why can't you be like we German dentist?" I couldn't even feign a faint smile at him. I pointed up vaguely with my right forefinger trying to indicate which tooth it was and for him to hurry up and get on with it as I hadn't all day to waste listening to his rabid ramblings.

"Ah yes you watch what I work", and a mirror was thrust into my right hand; with this his rubber hand disappeared out of my mouth.

"The last thing I want to see is what's going on in my mouth!" I pulled a false smile as I handed him back his mirror. He went straight back into it. "You English dentist. You fill and fill and fill tooth until nothing left. Vhy can't you be like ve Germans?"

I shrugged my shoulders in quiet submission, he had at least two metal objects in my mouth at this stage so I wasn't getting into any dispute with him.

"In Germany ve fill vonce, ya?"

My forehead wrinkled in pathetic agreement.

"Ve fill twice, ya?"

Just my luck I thought, first holiday in years, I drive the whole length of Europe and who do I run into in the south of Spain, none other than the son of Joseph Mengele. Visions of Dustin Hoffman sitting strapped into the dentist's chair with Laurence Olivier poking at his cavities danced through my mind. I had better sit exactly still.

"Then ve crown." I could feel a hint of exasperation in his voice. There's only one thing worse than being a dentist, I thought to myself, that is being an impatient dentist's patient.

"It is your National Health Service." I nodded gently and in as placatory a manner as I could muster but I haven't a lot of practice at acting dumb and subservient.

The rest of his conversation was in German to Helga or whatever her name was; she looked like your typical East German shot putter of old, big, blond and obviously ready to hit me a good hard smack if I didn't behave. Although years younger than him I found out after, she doubled

as his wife and trebled as a mother to three children of his. After some poking, some prodding, some blasting with air, some blitzing with a water jet, I departed from their whiter than white interior, clutching my prescription for real antibiotic for men and only fifty Euro the poorer for my experience.

Out into the wagen and the caring eyes of my family, who asked: "Are you okay now dad?" I smiled into the rear view mirror to them and off we headed to Mijas. It is not too many miles up the road and there was no point in anyone suffering along with me. We took the correct route up which isn't windy but goes straight up the mountain; yes I mean straight, third gear for most of it and down into second for the top part. There were a few places the children wanted to revisit and a few indispensables they needed to buy to take home for themselves and for others. The journey was no bother, the town is a lovely little place, so where better to go to forget the anger in my gum. Our first stop was a Farmacia where we handed in the prescription, received back our box of tablets, handed over four Euro and sixty cents and had our prescription handed back to us. Junkies at home would love this way of doing business. If by tomorrow morning the tablets have started to work, I think we'll try the prescription again in a Farmacia near the apartment, just to be sure for going through France.

Tomorrow, Wednesday, is our last day here in the apartment in the south of Spain, we'll be leaving very early on Thursday morning to do Spain in a single jump. I cannot say I am glad to be leaving, just as I cannot say that I am glad to be going home. Of the two I feel I've had my time and good out of this place for now and it is time to be moving along. I suspect I have travelled a short distance on the road to catching myself on, hopefully being a more relaxed, better-balanced person. I do expect it to be much easier to re-adjust myself to my new life when we return home because of the break. In that I have always told myself and shown myself I could achieve whatever I put my mind to then I expect no less of myself in my new existence, in having a less frantic and frenetic life.

The antibiotic tablets zonked me for a couple of hours while the family battered the molecules out of the water in the swimming pool. It has taken me another couple of hours to come round properly and we're all watching the long awaited and greatly anticipated dvd of JRR Tolkien's 'The Lord of the Rings'. I have to say that in the aftermath of the Harry Potter film the children have been on continuous countdown to the cinematic release of Tolkien's highly acclaimed book. What is immediately obvious is that JRR didn't grow up in the age and image of film as did J K Rowling who had the smarties to write what in essence is a script, which was easily transferred to film and not a great roaming novel of double epic proportion.

'Lord of the Rings' in film version is like the road up to Ronda, which winds this way and that and is uphill all the way; Rowling uses a motorway, a French one with plenty of excellent pit stops. In 'Lord of the Rings' it is not the action sequences, which hold the picture together, it is not the carefully balanced tension that binds it, the only thing that holds the film together is the music. With more twists and turns than the road up to Ronda I couldn't imagine this film being made in the days before computer graphics. After a couple of hours when concentration has lapsed for the umpteenth time it becomes an endurance test to see who can feign interest the longest. From the children's point of view the film was a big disappointment, it didn't work for them and I don't think it was because they knew this was their last family dvd sitting for the duration. Mind you, it's good to see Christopher Lee still retains a healthy interest in the dark and demonic side of our nature, he always was good for a laugh when they put a black cloak on him.

All is well in the world when your concentration is not consumed by a single, obsessive pain such as a toothache. Seven hours sleep last night was disturbed this morning before 8am by the poxy part of my troubled tooth deciding it had mustered enough strength during the night to begin a new attack. Up and a couple of tablets later I was sitting in the lounge dozing myself into a slumber of one and a half-hours. I am going to miss being able to lie about in my nags doing as little as is necessary to keep body and soul together. I hope I've broken the back on the old nutter that was me and have managed to learn to relax, not even learn to relax, but to relax, to walk away inside my head from all the nonsense. The holiday has certainly worked in that I feel better able to cope with the intricacies of life in the modern world, or post-modern world, or whatever as yet unspecified slot in time we are masquerading as existents in.

Wednesday it is, our last day hereabouts for quite some time and Caroline has been busy cleaning and sorting from early morning. Now we are all seated around the table on the patio having our al fresco breakfast of fruits of the locality, tea, toasts and whatever else in terms of cereal they don't want – it's the milk they blame.

So this is what people do, they relax. They go off on holiday and clear all the clutter out of their head so there is room for being, as well as for being nice, for being normal, for living a little. In the first place they probably haven't got themselves wound up like a taut elastic that's about to snap; they probably don't grind their teeth at night either so that this too is another problem area already happening; and so it goes on as you continue your stupidity and work too hard and before you know it you have irritable bowel whatever and blood pressure that's about to pop you into the ionosphere or stratosphere or whichever is furthest away. Stand back, take stock of your life, stop confusing the very straight–forward matter of living or not with the crowd of side issues. Take more time out, time off, time away, to give your head room to breathe. Bring back your smile, you sure as hell need it just as others need it too.

Not too many years ago we were taught society was made up of haves and have noughts; this, if ever it was the case, is no longer so. Society is made up of the dos and don'ts. Those who work for a living and those who don't. Unfortunately for the dos they are being squeezed by the don'ts from above as well as below. A large swathe of the population has been taught that the more useless you are, the more society will give you and look after you. Isn't that smart? At the same time as this there is a sizeable and growing proportion of those who would also rather not do but not do without at the other end of the 'social spectrum' whose wont it is to do nothing of constructive value by way of claiming it to be their birthright. The awful arrogance at both ends of our social spectrum means that on the one hand are those who are paid by others to do nothing and on the other hand are those who pretend to pay others so they can do nothing. These 'others' that both sets of non-functionaries look to for help so they can do nothing are we the working classes. We range from the well paid down to the not so well paid but the one thing we all increasingly have in common is that we have less and less time for ourselves. Demands of the job more than anything else is the big eataway here.

'Those lucky enough to have a job...'. We grew up with this stinging in our ears; but social equations are not mathematical sums, they don't add up and certainly not in the way governments, the social and economic legislators of the past century or two, have sought to keep and win votes with freebies and give-aways. All these bribes have added up and we, the real workers, are now paying a hefty price for social blackmail on the one hand and corporate blackmail on the other.

Back to reality! The children are returning from their last taste of the swimming pool here and I can feel Caroline's temper starting to simmer as she gets us all organised for leaving. She enjoys it all, it is just that the children do not respond quickly enough or expertly enough or they ask the wrong question in response to the unreasonable demand their mother has just made of them. Tempers are starting to fray again and one in particular.

We have just ended our deflationary period; we have been letting the air out of armbands, rubber rings (I suppose they must be made of plastic these days) floats, lielows and last but by no means least, all the Spanish air out of Stephen's boat which in itself was a fifteen minute ordeal for three of us. Letting out the air is not as easy an operation as it used to be because there is some sort of valve in the nozzle or nipple but Peter and Stephen very quickly picked up how to tweak this till it worked, a lesson which could prove invaluable to them later in life. Wind down is turning into wind up as things needing done don't keep pace with mind allocation for Caroline's top up of suntan, her trip to the pool already having had to be missed.

I am beginning to understand what the older generation means when it says it has never been so busy, that it hasn't a minute, since it retired.

It is nearly a quarter to two in the afternoon and we still haven't managed to have lunch yet. Isn't that great? Dribbling about has never seemed so time-consuming or been so interesting as it is on a foreign shore. There's no guilt attached here. No guilty feeling that comes from your car still sitting in the driveway after 9.15 in the morning. Stuff all that nonsense. There should be a feeling of utter and complete joy, a feeling of self fulfilment and self satisfaction at being able to lie in your snoozer for as long as you want; of getting up when your body announces it wants to and not having to jump to some preordained time schedule imposed by someone you otherwise wouldn't let anywhere near your life except that she, he or most probably it, helps keep you in the debt to which you have become ensnared.

I think we are leaving just in time. Rebecca has unceremoniously dethroned Emma off the sun lounger she had so meticulously positioned beside her mother. It definitely was unfair but the way I see it Rebecca's needs are much greater than Emma's and a bit of sun bonding between mother and eldest might do both some good before we hit the wagen trail tomorrow. Anyway, Emma has always the uncushioned option of a lie down; she knows she's beaten on this one so she's away in a huff to seek solace in the arms of Sarah, her twin. Caroline is determined to remain oblivious to everyone and everything for the short space of time her legs have left in direct sunshine. The only thing I can see that is going to stand in the way of Caroline and her quest for a golden glow is a strato cumulus or whatever formations of clouds take above this part of the globe and as we all know there is absolutely no chance of a cloud ever appearing around these parts at this time of year.

The twins have become masterful imitators of regional variations of the English accent. They have had a lot of practice with a lot of coming and going in the twenty-four apartments that make up the complex and the use of the pool, which is where Sarah and Emma have taken most of their lessons. A lot of the apartments around are rented out for the whole of the summer, perhaps for the whole of the year, for a couple of weeks at a time; with the size of our connection there would never be any time left over for others to enjoy the benefits it has to offer, whether paying or not. A different English regional variation in accent has moved

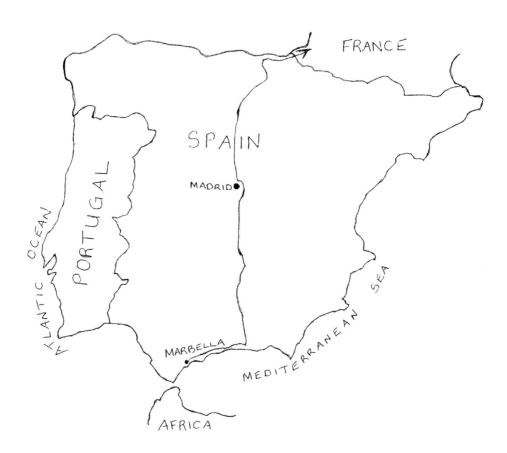

in next door again, very different judging by the broadcast of their voice and the simplicity of some of their tattoos; I think we might be leaving just in time. The thermometer is well up in the forties now.

The family has had its final outing this afternoon to Bela Modena where we had a nice long walk, quite a few nik-naks were bought for pressies - you know that last minute urge to make sure you have extra extra presents, just in case you've forgotten somebody important or, wait for it, in case one of the presents gets broken on the way home. When we went in for our McFlurrys for the children and cone each for Caroline and myself I realised that one of these delicious cones costs fifty cents, which is about thirty pence in our money back home which would buy you one of the skinniest, cheapest ice pops in any shop. I haven't seen very much that is dearer than back home, everything that matters is cheaper out here; if you worked at it you could live very very cheaply in Spain; now there's a thought.

Poor Caroline, the girl who didn't want to come to Spain in the first place now doesn't want to leave it and certainly not to go home even though that's over a week away yet. She's in love, perhaps not for the first time, perhaps not for the last time, in love not just with Spain and the sunshine and lifestyle this affords, but she is in love, really in love with her legs. She has become really attached to them, looks after them and cares for them in an unbelievable way, she even takes them with her wherever she goes and shows them off at any given opportunity. It all makes sense out here; sunshine and heat all day every day; time to do whatever you want whenever you want; small apartment with everything instead of a big house with too much; bathing suits that rinse out and dry within minutes; everyone has time and inclination to chip in and help with meals; swimming pool on your door step; beach around the corner; all the time in the world to enjoy yourself and every facility at your disposal to help you do so.

So we are off in the early hours of the morning, up through the centre of Spain, past Madrid, to the north coast of Spain, into France and thence to Bergerac for tomorrow evening. I'd better get a good night sleep.

Chapter Twelve

The Way Back

Nine hundred and three miles; on the road for fifteen hours and fifty minutes.

This is the morning after the drive before. It is Friday the 16th August and the second most important reason for remembering this date is that it is the anniversary of Elvis' death. The first and most important reason for any David Bowie fan remembering this date is that it is Caroline's birthday.

Happy birthday darling.

The drive back up through Spain yesterday didn't take it out of me in the way the drive down through Spain did because I didn't let it. On the first drive from Toulouse to the south of Spain I drove hell for leather, head down, ninety miles per hour, eyes radared on what was happening on the road ahead. For the return jaunt I knew I needed to drive in as relaxed a way as possible. I put the two armrests down and

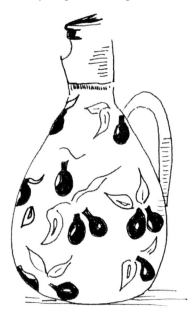

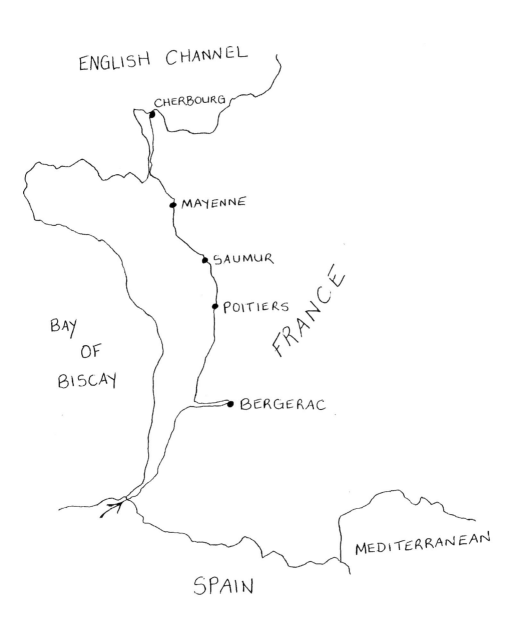

relaxed my elbows so that my two hands rested on the bottom of the steering wheel. Driving in this fashion at ninety miles per hour along motorways is easy peasy.

What is not so easy is when you decide to go into Bilbao in northern Spain for a bite of dinner at lunchtime. Bilbao is an enormous city and enormously difficult to get out of once you're off the motorway and then in the centre of chaos. When we made our escape we decided it would be a better idea to stop in San Sebastian which is a beautiful, beautiful city. The only problem was that it was a holy day or bank holiday or some other such sort of day when the whole of Spain takes the day off and, yes you've guessed it, heads for San Sebastian. They all got there before us so we couldn't even find a place to double park in the centre of town. Eventually we found our way out into the outskirts and yes, you've guessed it again, we found a McDonalds where we restocked our stomachs. Perhaps it didn't feel like the best McDonalds we've ever had because we were so hungry and had looked for it so long and hard and they were so busy because there was nowhere else open on the outskirts of town.

On and on we drove through the glorious vineyard invested back roads of the Dordogne until we finally reached our destination, it was around nine o'clock in the evening. Caroline went in with our tickets and had a stand up row with the owner who happened to be on desk duty at the time. He insisted that we needed four rooms and not the three that were booked because only two people were allowed in a room at a time, even though Caroline pointed him to the brochure which specifically states three to a room. It didn't matter, if we wanted three rooms, we had to take four. So, he was paid for his forth room, which is all he wanted and so he was happy. He must have been even happier to find we didn't use the forth room; strange that, especially when three of our rooms were adjoining and the forth was away on a different floor.

The Dordogne region has three main features going for it: sun, seed and soil. It has had the benefit of these three major elements over the past God knows how many centuries, the net result of which is riches aplenty and don't they know it and don't they show it. They show it in the beauty of their landscape and buildings, with nothing around these parts spoiled for the sake of a grant and a couple of temporary jobs. We haven't had much contact with the ordinary people but the shopkeepers show an enormous tendency to be ignorant and arrogant.

We breakfasted down by the river Dordogne in Bergerac this morning with real croissants again – the Spanish ones didn't have the same delicious meltdown quality – watching at swim the different sizes of fish, and as we ate our falling crumbs brought out the surprise of the day. A small lizard with its home in the cracks and crevices of the very high wall at the side of the river decided to come out and investigate us and enjoy some of our food away with him; he peeped back out from time to time to make sure we were dropping more crumbs for later. Very high are the walls along the banks of the river, very tall and proud stands the bridge, very far back up from the river stand the houses; car parks and walkways are all that is near the river. The reason is that during winter and despite the best efforts of grants and temporary jobs on a couple of dams up river, the level of the river rises by a minimum of between four and five metres, which is a lot of water passing through every second. In fact, they state that in 1783 the flooding was so high it washed the bridge away. Well, they should look on the bright side, at least it was clean when they got it back.

Presently we are picnicking on the outskirts of Sarlat, on the edge of a forest, with three low flying military aircraft shaking the leaves off the trees around us with their ground shaking manoeuvres.

On up the road not too many miles is Beynac which you have to see to believe. The castle stands with its own chapel at the top of a rock at least three hundred feet high accessed by way of very narrow little mini streets that form a magnificent settlement of houses, shops and buildings. All has been brilliantly restored to its thirteenth century splendour and provides a very exact picture of how a first rate settlement looked and functioned seven or eight hundred years ago; mind you, I don't think they had the luxury of so many ice-cream sellers then. At the base of this rock, across the very narrow main road, we sat along the riverside and ate our baguettes and drank our juices and fizz and watched at play the canoes and boats on the river Dordogne. There were at least fifty canoes with one, two and three people on board. It is a whole new world for the children to see a river being used and enjoyed by locals and holiday splashers for anything other than fishing. It was

delightful being able to chill out on the banks of the river watching my family enjoy watching the world enjoy itself.

After the long drive yesterday my head wasn't too bad today, headache was only a thirty per center which was not helped by the climb up and up and up to the castle, now that was one to make you sweat. Lying about, taking it easy down by the river provides great relief. The countryside of the Dordogne is brilliant, they even grow a lot of tobacco here and hang the leaves out in great big open wooden sheds to dry. Housing is as you would dream it to be, from castle to chateau to houses that have evolved with the needs of the people as well as being fashioned out of and into the landscape, there are very few examples around that have been penned on an architect's board. No blocks of flats here such as those that are so sinfully evident everywhere your eye travels in Spain. No Swiss influenced large roofed chalet type dwelling houses, which were prevalent in the Basque regions of Spain and France. This is dream country and people come here on holiday to confirm that dreams can and do come true, that's the positive polish on it; the reality is that these dreams only come true for those who are born into them, grow up living in them and thus know they are anything but a dream.

Dinner was a feast of eating and drinking and ice-creaming in a beautiful canal town. Eating spaghetti dishes and pizza after nine o'clock in the evening whilst sitting out on the restaurant terrace at the side of a quiet street in a little town where the only activity was stall holders booking their place for the morrow morning is what al fresco eating is all about. The children marvelled at the dining habits of others and at some of the extraordinary relationships children had with their parents where there was bullying, except in reverse. The children also marvelled at the absolute enormity of the meals we were served up and try as we might and most certainly did, there was no way on God's earth that we were ever going to finish them; but we sure did enjoy trying to.

What a night's sleep – not! We were so tired last night after our early departure and long drive we could have slept on a razor's edge. We are booked in for two nights into our four bedroom rip-off stop and tonight we notice, mainly through our lack of sleep, our bed is concave, the mattress is wafer thin and the room is so hot hot hot you could grow tomatoes on a commercial scale. Every half-hour, every twenty minutes, I watched the digital clock that stares out red eyed at the bottom of the portable television. Every other hour I was up drinking water or throwing cool water over my face and head to try and cool myself down enough to get back to sleep. It would work but only for about three minutes at a time and then I was back tossing and turning on the bed, as was Caroline all night. None of this seems to bother the children too much, who think it is all just wonderful and this is what hotels are really like, we must be too old or too spoiled or perhaps a bit of both. I'll not be sorry to leave this unconditioned hot house in an hour or two but I supposed I'd better get cleaned up first.

We are leaving Bergerac and heading for Poitiers. We are well into countdown now with four nights left in France, one in the boat and then we're on the road home. I have to say that after last night I am looking forward to getting my head back down on the coolness of my own pillow in the comfort of my own bed even though the purpose of this is to give the children a good time and that is what we will do to the very end. Is it just what you leave behind that you regard with most favour? Time will tell.

It is amazing. It's as if we drove through the countryside at home today; the hedgerows were thorn coming down with blackberries; the weeds, everything about the land was the same, apart from the size and vigour of the crops in the fields and the shapes of the houses. The tall crops growing in the fields are corns and the countryside is full of these healthy specimens along the back roads from Bergerac to Poitiers and these back roads are still as good as our main roads back home. We had a lovely day meandering our way through countryside as good as what we've been reared in except for the bonus of heat and sun and the advantages this brings in its trail. There were still a few chateaux about only not as numerous as before or as well defended.

Onto Poitiers where the hotel we were booked into was in the same grand theme park as Futuroscope. They must half taken half the local countryside, wiped it clear and clean of every building that ever stood on it and then built built built hotel after hotel on an enormously grand scale and with all sorts of other eateries and playeries around. It was very handy being able to park the wagen when we arrived and not having to move it until we left for our next destination at the end of the following day. It meant we got some good hefty walks in but we enjoyed that. The evening we arrived we took a good walk to an entertainment complex not too far distant and inside there was a rock and roll style restaurant. Some of the children ordered chicken dishes, the rest, including Caroline and myself, ordered their biggest, beefiest burgers with chips and salad. The waiter taking the order was Dutch and his English was excellent. Caroline's last words to him were: "Well done. Make sure the burgers are well done."

There is a chance I suppose that he misinterpreted what she was saying and he may have put no pass on the words 'well done' except that maybe she was giving him a pat on the back for his standard of spoken English being so high. Out came the plates full of burgers, chips and salad, and we bit grandly into their deliciousness and just at that point where the burger retreats from the grip of your teeth and catches the corner of your eye, and then the full concentrated stare of both your eyes, you see that it is red, running rancid roaring red inside a slightly cooked exterior. Yuk! The bloody burgers were just that, bloody uncooked. Despite my mind's eye's better judgement I ate mine, Peter ate his, whilst the rest of them picked and dabbed so much at theirs' they seemed to send back more on their plates than had come out. The uneating experience was not cheap and to add insult to injury there was a fifteen per cent surcharge on top of the high prices.

McDonald's is too unbloody good for us all in future. It is strange that there the children get plenty to eat, they don't leave even a sesame seed behind them and it costs less than one third of this eating fiasco.

We walked round to the enormous Futuroscope complex to get our bearings for the morning and to buy our tickets in so we wouldn't have to queue; also to get a guide book on the place to find out where to go, where not to go.

Thank goodness the Campanile hotel is a good one, it's a good big one anyway with one hundred and ninety-three rooms, unlike last night's kip; so, a good nights sleep ahead for us which we'll need if we are to make a good go at Futuroscope tomorrow.

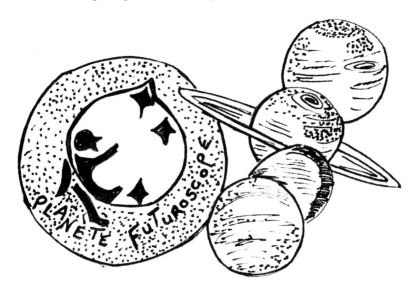

In that Disneyland is a stupid place, Futuroscope is a stupid place for people who think they're smart – the French. This is the French doing what they do best; being French. Futuroscope is the French taking the Yanks on at what the Yanks do best but adding a bit of Gallic flair and flavour, as you would expect, and failing brilliantly. It is like the French taking the Americans on at sport but agreeing to a battle of the nations over a game of American football instead of rugby. When I say that the French fail brilliantly at whatever Futuroscope is meant to be I mean that the size, scale and architecture of Futuroscope is brilliant, it is just that it is let down by its content. The reality of what Futuroscope

113

actually amounts to could have been put into one of its buildings which would provide visitors with an insight into the way the world is going in terms of how scientists see the way ahead taking shape.

History. France is what it has been which is its history, which is what most visitors come to France for. I'm sure if they put their collective mind to it they could have one of these magnificent structures housing a peep show with the French Revolution and its lead on into the wonders of the Napoleonic age. As well as French history there's geography, inventions, the arts – you name it, I'm sure the French could put together a wonderful interactive section on each. Giving people an angle on tomorrow's world is all very fine and dandy but most visitors want to taste France and adding the extra dimensions of France then as well as now as well as the future would prove to be an irresistible combination.

Success in this game is something that can only be measured in numbers attending and there were no great numbers drawn to this magnificence. The car park was around a quarter full, there were no great crowds wandering round or queuing, apart from a few of the more popular rides later on. Take away the fancy name, take away the fancy buildings, take away all the razzmatazz connected with the place, what it amounts to is films, some in 3D, bumpety bump rides, amusement parks and games, all designed to take your money. Call it what you will, dress it up in fancy whatever, it is designed and laid out so when you exit a lot of the theme areas, you have to pass through a video games stall designed to lighten your pocket before you get to your next theme area which you have already paid for.

The French regard of themselves, their arrogance, is probably what has helped maintain their splendid isolation at the heart of Europe. Their inimitable style is what has kept them being what they are; where they are in terms of being at the heart of European society is where they always have been and with a bit of luck, where they always will be. If the French are at the heart then the Germans are at the head and so it will be until the French learn to take themselves a little less seriously. We are the visitors who are coming from all over Europe, from all over the world and are pouring our hard earned into French pockets and in return we are not asking the French to be grateful, heaven forbid; we are

not asking for anything by way of thankfulness, perish the thought; we are looking for a bit of common courtesy, thank you. In Futuroscope, for instance, you could put up a few signs in English, perhaps even print a few handouts in English. At the moment the only signs in English and German as well as French, are the warning signs and we all know that these are only there to cover your collective ass for insurance purposes.

It is a mistake to compete with Disneyland on its bright lights, all image and no substance style terms. Disneyland has the advantage of the playful, carefree corner of our brain being tuned into it from a very young age by way of the films we watch at the cinema, on television and thence that we buy on video and dvd and play over and over again. Disneyland has a hold on both the head and the heart of every punter who enters its gates. Our children were over the moon about going to it and they almost had to be dragged away from it even though they were emotionally drained and physically exhausted; it is the one place they insist on telling others they have been to. Just as Disneyland was the highlight on the way down through France so Futuroscope was the highlight on the way back up and the children were looking forward to it a lot, they did enjoy their time in the place, but that is it. They talk and talk of Disneyland and also in terms of when they are next going to visit it but there is no mention of Futuroscope.

Number one rule in life is to play it smart but in order to do the smart thing the French are first of all going to have to swallow hard.

From a very young age I was taught that pride comes before a fall. The French undoubtedly do have an awful lot to be proud of but real nobility comes with inclusiveness, not inviting you in only to ignore you then.

I nearly forgot to mention, while we were in Futuroscope it rained for a couple of hours, raindrops were falling on our heads and on our clothes, an experience we have not had the delight of since last we were at home. I suppose we'd better start getting used to it again. I also neglected to mention the queuing system in Futuroscope. The closest in kind I can think of closed down at home about twenty-five years ago although a few still survive in the larger market towns that serve some of the outlying country localities. The metal used in these open but roofed queuing systems was not of the polished stainless steel variety used in Futuroscope. The main difference is that at home they are used in the cattle market whereas Futuroscope uses them for humans.

Isn't that sweet?

Driving along the back roads of France is a wonderfully absorbing and relaxing experience. Today we had the comparatively short distance to travel from Poitiers to Saumur, the roads are based on the good old fashioned idea that the quickest way from A to B is a straight line between the two which means easy driving, which means I had the chance to rest my head back and look around me. On the way back up France I have had the opportunity to notice cars I haven't seen back home since the 1970s and 1980s. Talbots and Simcas, Renaults and Citroens; the Renaults are numbered anything from four to twenty-one and there have been lots of older cars such as a beautiful and appropriately named Renault Caravelle, a convertible of course. In the country areas especially, the old cars appear to have been carefully parked at the side of barns or laid up in numbers of three to five just off the sides of main roads but still in full view of passing traffic; large adorable ornaments on display. The weather must be a lot kinder to old vehicles hereabouts, or perhaps it's that they kept the good ones for themselves and sent the Monday and Friday cars over la Manche.

One of the places we drove through yesterday was a name. It was supposedly a village or small town but it wasn't really in that the estate of which it owes its name is much larger in size and certainly much grandeur than the town itself. The estate is high walled and the number of entrances we passed would not have been out of place in terms of style and grander in a boulevard in Paris. The name of the estate as the name of the village is Richelieu and it would be a cardinal sin for anyone to change it; the boys were disappointed there was no sign of any of the musketeers.

A pleasant night's sleep and you are set up for anything during the day, you can take anything on. When the sun is up and at you and it is only nine o'clock in the morning then the day is looking good for you and now we're further north and the heat is not going to melt my hat onto my head or my back to the seat of the wagen, then it's my sort of day. Tonight's stop is in Mayenne, tomorrow night's in Cherbourg and next port of call after that fills me with the joy of the road home and seeing mother, Tom and the rest of the family again and getting settled into my new and more relaxed way of living and being. Whoops! Just when I thought things were going brilliantly Caroline informs me today is designated a day of sun and shops; how I love to hear that, not quite.

We had our normal travelling breakfast by the river in Saumur, of baguettes, bananas and water out in the cool of a shaded morning which is about as healthy an eat as you'll get. We had to move on then because the town hadn't woken up yet and it was now ten o'clock and, to Caroline's horror, it wasn't due to waken for another three hours. We stopped at the side of the straight line between Chateau-Goutier and Laval eating the delicious remainders of our patisserie purchases from earlier.

We have arrived in our penultimate stop in France, Mayenne. It is an uncharacteristically characteristic town of middle France in that it has a few different and decent buildings, a few decent shops, ordinary countryside and the rest is plain, working France although I haven't seen too much evidence of the French at work.

Of the two countries, France and Spain, France is by far the lovelier but for a family holiday the way we did it in Spain is the way to do it. Take your darling to France and enjoy its beauty, its glory together. France does not appear to do anything on the cheap and therefore it doesn't allow anyone else a cheap ride but we all know it is worth paying extra for quality so long as this is needed and appreciated. Children do not need or appreciate quality and with six children this becomes a big expense. Spain on the other hand is cheap and very cheerful and a damn good place it is to have a holiday for whatever size of family or pocket you might have. Spain has had the advantage of providing us with a palatial base but this aside Spain wins hands down on the holiday front. As with everything in life it depends on what your needs are and for our lot it wasn't a great idea living out of a suitcase with one night stops, it wasn't a great idea going to national monuments, but it was a superb idea to have a swimming pool for them to flounce about in all day. It is unfair to put France and Spain together, they are two totally different destinations and wrong therefore to try to compare them; let me say that there is a lot to see and enjoy in France whilst Spain is a great place to go to enjoy yourself.

After checking into our lovely Campanile hotel on the outskirts of Mayenne we drove back into town and parked down by the riverside.

On our way up into the town centre we took the circuitous route round by the second bridge and up into the old quarter. Driving around the town earlier Caroline's eye had obviously spotted a couple of shops she was interested in so on our way to the restaurant we had to do a hit on a couple of jewellers in one of which she nabbed a nice ring as a birthday present. By the end of the dealings we were absolutely starving so we all rushed to the restaurant and comfortably positioned ourselves at the tables. The waiter came out to serve us, only drink, there was no food being served until seven o'clock. Broken, desperate, starving with hunger, we shuffled off up the street into a small park at the side of the chateau with its embattlements overlooking the banking down to the road one hundred feet below and on down to the river.

The park had a small but open play area which amused the younger ones while Caroline, myself and the older ones sat on a bench chatting of where and when until we saw the magnificent variety of trees included a couple of horse chestnut. Although not quite ripe, as with much else in life it's the getting that brings the purest sense of delight, the end product bringing with it an element of self-satisfaction. So we hunted down a few of the larger chestnuts which were just within arms' reach until a few fatter and higher delights I managed to cleave from their safe height by way of using the camera in its case as a type of modern day ball and chain. When we began our chestnutting exploits the solitary bell of a nearby church sounded calling the faithful to evening prayers, it was ten to seven; we were still there in the middle of our exploits when the bell again sounded saying prayers had begun, it was seven o'clock.

Quick-stepping it back to the restaurant to resume our rightful places at the tables we earlier had to depart, it wasn't long before pizzas of different varieties arrived in front of us for devourment. It was here, this very evening, in the town of Mayenne in France that Stephen Black became a man; for here, in front of the whole town – well, those who glanced a look – Stephen ate his first full pizza. This he downed with a load of chips, washed away with Coca-Cola and topped off with yet another Carte d'Or ice-cream. What a delicious evening! Back to the hotel then for more drinks and goodies and the children then settled down in their respective rooms to watch 'The Nutty Professor" in

French; isn't Eddie Murphy talented!

Do not book in anywhere in France and that goes for even the cooler north unless it has air conditioning. Last night it was definitely cooler up in these more northerly parts of Mayenne but it is not enough. Broken sleep after lying for over an hour trying to get to sleep does not leave you feeling on top of the world for heading at cross angles over to Le Mont St Michel this morning before straight up the west coast toward our last stop in Cherbourg tonight. It would be more than amiss of us not to visit Le Mont when we are not too far away from it, as it is one place I've always had in my head to see.

It must be something to do with their age or maybe it is tied in with being on holiday but at around the same age as the boys I remember having the same competitions during holidays as they are having now. Staring competitions are obviously still on the go some thirty years later despite all the gameboy, video games, computer games, mobile telephones and the like. I would venture to suggest they are better at it than we were because they've had a lot more practice with all their electronic gadgetry; all we had to stare at was the irrepressible mirror. So modern magictry can only take a young one so far, when they enter their teenage years it's the same as it ever was, the individual against himself.

Just before midday we joined the queue to enter the car park; four Euro is very little to ask to park on a sandy field for as long as you need when it is expertly laid out and run by guys with walkie-talkies, and there were hundreds and hundreds of other vehicles all looking in too. Le Mont Saint Michel is truly a wonderful sight, created by God but bettered by man, so just think what the Disney corporation could do with it, for a start the church at the top would make a wonderful palace for Cinderella. The car parking in the wide open fields would remind you of Glastonbury only for middle class culture vultures who for the rest of their mediocre lives will be able to say: "Ah yes, Le Mont, I was there, very impressive but...". When Caroline and Rebecca finally decided on what is most suitable to wear on an occasion such as this we were off on our hike into the town.

It's a feast of a rock! Just as Gilbraltar is a shitty little carbuncle at the foot of Spain so Le Mont Saint Michel is what becomes of a similar sized and shaped lump of rock when the French get their hands on it. It is a

masterpiece of vertical architecture, which starts with lowly houses and what are now hotels, restaurants and shops surrounded by the first battlements. There is only one embanked way into the town when the tide is in and in former times there was probably a drawbridge there instead. Narrow, very narrow cobble streets rise up in a winding manner through the next levels of old prison and what are now museums and more battlements until on up at the uppermost level is the spectactularly impressive church. Today, and I'd say it is the case for every day throughout the summer, the place is bunged with people, it is impossible to walk quickly, it is impossible to walk slowly, you have to shuffle along as if your trousers are down round your ankles but even then you are stopping more than you are starting.

Eejits with dogs ended up carrying their hairy crappers in their arms; eejits with prams ended up abandoning them on the lower reaches and carrying their baldy crappers in their arms. Everyone was happy, smiling, sweating, phoning, texting, buying, eating, smoking, talking, pushing, photographing, watching, laughing, climbing, drinking – it is such a busy place you have to be aware of where other people are in terms of inches and not feet because there is no room for error. Sometimes crowds as busy and pushing and shoving and slow as this can bring out the worst in people but not here, in fact the opposite; whatever it was people were meant to be doing, they were all very happy almost doing it. The queue to get out of Le Mont St. Michel was longer than the queue in and this was over four hours later and they were still queued right out to get in.

On up the coastal road to Gr. Gr. Granville as Ronnie Barker would call it. Granville is an exceptional town, well meaning and business like with the Atlantic waves washing the tan off the hardened swimmers. After going through the town with Caroline and the girls making a thorough inspection of every suitable commercial establishment, we took our ice-creams for a walk along the promenade. A beautiful sun-burning early evening it was as we walked past the long line of sunbathers sitting outside their numbered little palaces. When I say 'little palaces' more emphasis should be put on the 'little' than the 'palaces'. The reality is that more than sixty double wardrobes had been set down along one side of the promenade and then painted white; perhaps they are tardis-like and of magnificent proportion inside; judging by the size of some of the users they would certainly need to be. On our walk back up through the town we tried every appropriate looking restaurant to see if we could get something to eat but there was nothing doing, the earliest any outlet could manage was six o'clock and it was not quite five o'clock yet.

Onwards and upwards we travelled through what could well have been countryside from home if the sun hadn't shone so much. We didn't bother to stop at any of the more and more numerous American War Cemeteries, in fact, we didn't bother stopping until we reached Coustances. We parked in the square in front of the church and headed down a side street to a pizzeria, which came a very tasty second to the one in Paris for an absolutely delicious evening. Everything about the place was clean, beautifully and tastefully decorated and the pizza menu was second to none, in terms of toppings and taste the pizzas were truly magnificent.

On the drive up to Cherbourg after our meal we were entertained by a sweet little bird which hit the bonnet, did a double flip and side turn, bounced off the windscreen with the same look of surprise and impending horror as appeared on Caroline's face, back flipped a couple of times and performed an excellent forward roll over the top of the wagen before completing the sequence with a superb pirouette as it landed a bit too smartly on the tarmac behind, but just in time for the car following to end any chance it may have had of leading a severely disabled life.

It wasn't too difficult to find the Kyriad hotel, just keep focus and you eventually get there. So, we're in Cherbourg, happily ensconced in our hotel rooms with our last night in France ahead of us, followed by a day in town before setting sail at six o'clock tomorrow evening local time. Caroline will have to make sure she has a couple of 'Sea Legs' tablets in her before boarding. Hopefully these will cure her wibbily-wobbliness.

D-day has arrived as we join the exodus out of here. Cherbourg is a big city but we'll see a bit of it before we head for the ferry this afternoon; so far what has distinguished Cherbourg from the rest of France is the fact it is the first city, town or village we have seen with a statue to Napoleon Bonaparte in any position, prominent or not. He sits resplendent on his charger in a high profile area down by the marina end of the docks. Memories and a sense of history must improve the further north you go.

It is not yet eight in the morning and Caroline has everyone up and at it so determined is she for us not to waste our last day in France. At the moment my feelings lie with the bed I'm in which has provided one of the better nights of sleep of recent days but I suppose I'd better be up and at it. After walking into an empty and closed Cherbourg this morning, eating a breakfast of croissants on the hoof, we did a quick turn around, headed back to the hotel only to stop in a supermarket just up from it to replenish our stock of goodies and necessaries for our journey home. Off then we headed to a town not too far distant called Valognes, another sleepy French town where most of the establishments were closed and those which weren't closed from twelve noon to two-thirty or twelve-thirty to three o'clock and only stayed open until seven in the evening. Aren't they a smart people? Who else would think up a timetable such as this and could then get away with it in business? We did manage to find a pizzeria open and enjoyed too early a feed; I don't think it was too big a feed for Rebecca and Thomas who managed to order and only half eat their pizzas which had some sort of creme in them, yeah, a bit too saucy for my liking too.

We made our way over to a quiet park, well it was quiet until we got there, for the children to go mad in and for Caroline and myself to enjoy the fruits of someone else's labour with a cup of tea and a pastry each; Caroline's was apple something or other, mine had slices of pear in a sweet jam over a soft, spongy base surrounded by a crisp pastry shell. Sheer tasty delight that only the French patisseries go in for in a decent way. After lazing about here for the guts of an hour we drove back to Cherbourg, to McDonald's, where Mc Flurrys were the order of the day and along with these, drinks and toilets were enjoyed by all.

Now we are off to catch the ferry.

Chapter Thirteen

Return

There are fifteen lines in the queue for the ferry and we are sitting at the very front of line twelve waiting for the off from the cheery chap who scoots about all the lines seemingly very happy with his lot in work, talking away to the occupants of the vehicles as well as to whoever happens to be on the other end of his walkie talkie. He points at us, puts his hand up as I thrust her into first gear and then he tells us to wait; tears off on his red scooter to a hut over by one side and then he returns straight away, holds his right hand aloft and waves us on. We are back on the Normandy, the ferry that had the distinction of bringing us over here in the first place. Our cupboards are in exactly the same place as before only on the opposite side of the corridor.

Sardines have my shallowest sympathy; I am lying on my lower bunk bed trying to write, which is a difficult enough task but not quite as difficult, I would venture to suggest, as getting to sleep is going to be tonight. Caroline is not at all happy, her 'Sea Legs' are obviously working so her claustrophobia has kicked in instead. I responded with my no nonsense bit because there is no point in taking any other approach as there is nothing I can do about the size of the cabin. I can turn the wee knob over by the door to make the cabin cooler or warmer but there is no way I can make it any bigger.

We didn't have to wait long before boarding and the boat left in reasonable time which was only about fifteen minutes late. The sea is very calm, thank God. Before we went to the pictures we had our tea up in one of the cafeteria areas with our flask, bottles of juice, baguettes, bananas, slices of chicken and ham; it wasn't very long into this holiday we learnt that if you go out anywhere with eight, you have to bring your own foodstuffs with you.

Back up on deck and the children counted eight container ships in our vicinity; it was lovely in that great healthy manner catching the evening breeze over the sea but the females in our company had other ideas as to just how good the bracing sea air was for them. We went down to the cinema, as it was almost time for the eight o'clock showing of Star Wars II: Attack of the Clones. Well, what can I say except that it passed a reasonable two hours and fifteen minutes and that was the main intention of it. My first tasting of Star Wars was whenever it was first released in or around 1977 when Siobhan, Tom, myself and cousin Nicola went to the Palace picture house at the bottom of Shipquay Street and departed afterwards back across Guildhall Square laughing and asking of each other: "What the heck was that all about?" I never really got into this genre of film, it was all a bit too unreal, unbelievable for me, not quite cowboys and Indians.

There, I knew it was possible to sleep on the parcel shelf of a bus, that's what it was like. The crossing was so smooth it would have been impossible not to sleep, except for the rising temperature level as the night wore on. I kept having to rise to increase the cool intake air valve firstly at 2.20am; at 5.20am myself, Peter and Stephen discussed the merits of a very early rise and decided it best to lie down again and try to get another hour out of the night. We next woke at 7.20am well pleased with our night-time endeavours and having to waken Thomas who had the good sense to sleep through it all.

Everyone is cleaned, refreshed and sitting up enjoying our good healthy breakfast in the cafeteria area, setting ourselves up nicely for the day's pleasant endeavours. We'll go up on deck shortly to see what Thursday morning has on offer for us. Hopefully the captain will announce shortly that we made good progress in the calm of the night waters.

I almost forgot to mention, I found out how the boys had a relatively good night's sleep last night; they had bought themselves a big bar of Toblerone yesterday evening on board the ship's shop so they each had that to snuggle up to comfort them in their dreams.

The captain has told us we are due to arrive at eleven o'clock which is three hours short of the suggested travel time as stated in their literature; it is probably necessary in sea-faring terms to do this not only because you are covered if this is the time it takes in poor seas but also because you please your passengers enormously when you do make good time.

Ah, our first sighting of home soil in about a month. Well, not quite soil, it's only a lump of rock with a light-house stranded on top. I hope it never had a resident lighthouse keeper in days of old. The children are now in a state of great excitement with a proper sighting of real land, of hills and beaches and houses. Stephen has been jumping up and down for more than five minutes now, I think he probably expects to see his granny Gorman waiting for him as soon as he steps onto land. The poor boy has missed her enormously, he hasn't shut up about her since we arrived in France one month ago. Nobody really mattered that much for Peter to miss, there was food and goodies aplenty in France and Spain and France again. Thomas missed his friends he claimed from time to time. I think he more missed the opportunities associated with being with his friends and the inevitable contact with girls this brings. Rebecca seems happy so long as there are shops and more shops and mirrors aplenty; it doesn't matter that her money ran out in no time at all, she knew the well had not run dry, and quite right she is too. The twins, Sarah and Emma, well, they think every day is a big adventure and they are correct. Caroline has enjoyed it all brilliantly, we are mature enough to know life holds a few hiccups for us along the way.

The road home was a bit on the slow side, in fact, a bit on the snails pace side if you compare it with the motorways of France and Spain. Everytime we got a bit of speed up in the wagen it seemed we had to stop again for roadworks. Perhaps this is a sign that things are improving.

It is day two after our return home. Let me explain.

When we reached home we called first at my mother's, nobody in so no change there, the golf course is rarely closed. We moved on up to Caroline's mother and father's house which is also no distance from our own. After the pleasantries and half a cup of tea for me and a glass of wine for Caroline Mr & Mrs Gorman informed us our house had been broken into and vandalised a few weeks previously. What? Some little blaggards, we don't yet know their names and number, at around three-thirty early one Sunday morning smashed twenty-two window panes at the back of our house, smashed their way into the utility room where they obviously partied in their own inimitable fashion by drinking a couple of bottles of plonk that were lying out there and then smashing and wrecking as much as they could manage. Thankfully they couldn't smash their way into any of the rest of the house. They tried also to smash their way in the front door but when they couldn't they turned their attention on Caroline's Caravelle, smashing the back window, the wing mirrors, denting panels, and trying unsuccessfully to smash front windows, thereby leaving a lot of scrapes and scratches instead. Generally, they caused a shit load of damage and left a hell of a mess.

Not that we saw any sign of it.

Tom, his wife Mary and their children along with Mr & Mrs Gorman did sterling work and had the place cleaned and almost as if nothing had been vandalised. New panes of glass were in and everything cleaned up as best they could.

This is the first time we've ever had any sort of nonsense of even an attempted break in kind. It is not a nice thing to happen. We tell ourselves it is to be expected in this day and age, that there is a lot of this type of behaviour going on. It is words like these that make this almost acceptable. It is not acceptable. It never will be acceptable. It is therefore incumbent upon every member of society from the judiciary right down to us ordinary yolks to play a part in stamping out any and all anti-social behaviour. Zero tolerance is the only approach.

All of this has put a different edge on coming home. While it was certainly not for the best it gave us something immediate and different to work on, to worry about. It takes a while to get over the motley feelings from the initial want to get the blaggards who did it, to finding ways of thanking those who helped clear up the mess, to dealing with the detail of sorting things out properly and making the house more secure. One of our first 'must dos' is to set up the alarm so that it is put on every time we leave the house. Anyway we're back, this blip will be washed away soon enough and we will then be better able to concentrate on being whatever we're meant to be, whatever that might be. The holiday, for whatever else it was worth, appears to have done its job with regards my attitude to work and my former ties to the filling station. My head has been won over, I now just have to work at the tightness in my chest with regards it all but time will sort that out too.

The children think it is brilliant to be back home and it must be for they don't have to come back to the nonsense that is always waiting for adults, and it is generally centred around work and the other little intricacies of life. Every opportunity they have the children are out and away through the gates to play with their cousins and friends. Rebecca's first request on our return home was for a phone card. A ten pound Vodaphone card was duly supplied and she hasn't left the intrepid little device out of her hand, her left thumb working overtime trying to keep apace with her thoughts and as she stops to let her thumb relax messages float in from the ether and land miraculously on her screen. The telephone hasn't cooled, the front door bell hasn't stopped ringing, the back door hasn't stopped clicking closed. A swimming pool is obviously only a temporary replacement for a whole host of friends and now they have left the swimming pool behind in Spain they have their host of friends to enjoy life with instead.

I must say that if this is what it is like to be relaxed, it is very civilised. It is Sunday morning and I haven't jumped up out of bed, dived out to work and grabbed a cup of tea and a couple of biscuits for breakfast whilst working flat out at sales, cashing up, restocking, ordering and the multitudinous number of other jobs you do to run a business successfully while at the same time having little or no regard for you own good health and well-being.

The first difference I have noticed in being around the family much more is that I have to indulge them each a lot more in my attentions. The older ones especially are coming and telling me little things, trivia, about friends, school, teachers, neighbours, relations, goldfish, toast, in fact all the thought processes and issues which are real and matter enormously to them. Possibly it is upon these little issues that the bigger ones, which are undoubtedly to come, are built. Perhaps these little listenings are my test, my test of trueness toward my children which they are subconsciously absorbing and if I successfully negotiate myself over these insignificances I will be allowed to progress onto the much bigger issues and problems when they arrive. Children are always looking for friends, perhaps the biggest and most important friends are those at home who protect themselves by continually pretending to be parents. Hopefully the most important element to come out of my recognition of self in terms of work and life is to come in developing a meaningful, understandable, workable and genuine relationship with my children.

I have learned Rebecca has a quiet sadness about her and only truly comes to life when she has one or more friends with her. I have learned

Thomas is in a great hurry to grow up emotionally. I have learned Peter has a beautiful laugh. I have learned Stephen wants to be with me more and more. I have learned Sarah and Emma got on better with their life with me around less as they had learned how to run rings round their mother.

Until now I had regarded myself as being everything to them. I was their father after all. I told them what to do and they understood the seriousness of this and did it. I was the great provider; I gave them everything they needed and in return they were obedient. I was their chauffeur, gardener, handyman, sometime cook and certainly bottlewasher. The list is endless but what were my children to me?

Individuals in there own right? – No chance.

Individuals in my right? – Not quite yet.

That was then, this is now and now they are starting to come into their own in their own right; now they are beginning to mature, they are starting to think for themselves and it won't be too long before they are fully doing for themselves. As they develop I will continue what I have begun in terms of reassessing and re-establishing my role, function and relationship with them. I have to remember that I am the grown-up who has to keep developing, keep changing who he is for the changing needs of his children.

What hasn't changed is that the children want the good times to continue. Aren't they the wise ones? For the first number of nights back home the children had it in their heads to come and sit with Caroline and myself in the lounge for the evening instead of their normal routine of them and theirs watching whatever was suitable in the living room. Normally this didn't last too long because somebody or other would call for one or all of the older ones and off they would shoot for an evening's entertainment in the street and in and out of the houses. It took them a few nights to fall back into their own space and out of our space and by now they are back in the way of their own way of being themselves both inside and outside the house.

I keep asking myself what does a good father do, what does a good father don't? A good dad does what needs to be done before the children get to think that it is what they want. A good father doesn't share his burdens with his children. Children's troubles should be aired and shared, adult's should not be heard by children.

Keep giving of yourself, what you are, what you have, to your children. Give them all the little things as well as all the big things. Give them a life they are going to treasure for always and which they will emulate and perhaps better when they are of an age and stage. Most especially most of all give them all the things you wanted when you were that age, all the things you got but more than this, all the getting you feel you missed out on.

Learn to say "Yes."

In the short space of time since the beginning of summer I know I have come a long way; I had gone as far as I was prepared to go along my old way and I was determined to deal with the one and only thing in my life which is real and means anything, my family. Hopefully the children will feel the good of the change as I have, time will tell.

Oh yes, it took us three thousand, eight hundred and thirty miles to get to the south of Spain, do our doings and get back home again.